W9-BCR-626

MINNESOTA DRAMA EDITIONS • EDITED BY TYRONE GUTHRIE

ANTON CHEKHOV

THE CHERRY ORCHARD

A Play in Four Acts

translated by

TYRONE GUTHRIE and LEONID KIPNIS

MINNEAPOLIS • THE UNIVERSITY OF MINNESOTA PRESS
IN ASSOCIATION WITH THE MINNESOTA THEATRE COMPANY

PRINTED IN THE UNITED STATES OF AMERICA

Library of Congress Catalog Card Number: 65-22809

All inquiries concerning performing rights (professional, amateur, and stock) should be addressed to the translators' representative: The Minnesota Theatre Company Foundation, 725 Vineland Place, Minneapolis, Minnesota 55403

Published in Canada by the Copp Clark Publishing Co. Limited, Toronto

TABLE OF CONTENTS

The Cherry Orchard

ABOUT THIS SERIES

BY TYRONE GUTHRIE

THE INTENTION of the University of Minnesota Press and the Minnesota Theatre Company is to make available in this series a number of important plays, written in languages other than English, on which we feel that a new translation would throw a new light, which would therefore make them more interesting and lively to the reader. There are very few important plays, whether in French, German, Russian, Spanish, Italian, or the Scandinavian languages, which have not been translated into English. But too often these translations have been made by fluent linguists with no feeling for the musical, as opposed to syntactical, qualities either of the original text or of English; or else no very clear understanding of the author's intention; or else no sense of theatre.

An accurate literal translation is not enough. For instance, a Russian writer will make a character say "My heart is unspeakably oppressed" or "My soul is filled with dark forebodings." Now in the English language an analogous character in an analogous situation will say "I feel depressed" or "I am anxious." We are chary, where Russians are prodigal, in referring to our hearts and souls.

Likewise a Scandinavian writer will say "Here comes School-Principal Relling, who has already arrived on the ferry-boat from Hogstrand and who, after attending the meeting of the Municipal School Board, will eventually return on the evening ferry-boat to Pigstrand." Such dialogue could, and does, occur in a Scottish play, because Scottish and Scandinavian minds move with a not dissimilar rhythm and logic. Facts, the exact sequence of time, cause and effect are important. There is no time for exaggeration or nonsense; or even for comment, unless it is strictly relevant. Elsewhere, in warmer, slacker climes, in societies less sternly devoted to the pursuit of truth and righteousness, and where, perhaps, there is more demand for fun and more patience with frivolity, information will be conveyed in a more disorderly, but, conceivably, more amusing and allusive manner.

I believe that it is the translator's business to try to find a way in which the speeches may seem in English to be plausible utterances of each particular character, and yet not entirely to lose the feeling of the original environment. This involves compromise. In Ibsen the characters ought, I believe, to suggest their Scandinavian environment, the weather, what those tight, powerful, censorious, little communities do to their inhabitants, but at the same time they must seem to English-speaking readers, audiences, or actors to be talking like real people. It is partly a matter, negatively, of avoiding words and phrases which are associated with another period or another environment—"O.K.," for instance, "blow up a storm," or "step on the gas"; partly a matter, positively, of finding rhythms, idioms, constructions, which are characteristic of spoken English. This often means substituting paraphrase for a literal translation.

Clearly, there can be no hard and fast rules. There never can be in art. It is a matter of the translator's taste, tact, integrity, and feeling for the music of speech and the relation of speech to character. I do not see how anyone can translate dialogue, whether in play or novel, unless he has a talent for, and if possible experience of, acting; the speeches must be "heard" so that the sentence is shaped to be speakable, with emphasis where it should be, with easy and expressive rhythm, changes of pace, possibilities for pause . . . in short, the translator must hear and feel each line of dialogue. Its music is just as important as its meaning—is, in fact, inseparable from its meaning.

Prose plays are easier to translate than plays in verse, where the style of the original is very much part of the content. It is hardly to be expected that rhyming verse will not lose incredibly in translation.

The work of some authors, apparently, translates rather easily into some languages, less easily into others. Shakespeare has never been very popular in France, largely because no satisfactory French translator has yet appeared. In Germany and in Russia, on the other hand, he is more frequently played, and more widely admired, than in the English-speaking world. And this is largely because satisfactory, actable translations exist, and have existed for many years.

The English-speaking theatre has been especially ill served in the matter of translations from the German. How seldom an English version of a German classic is produced! I have never seen a performance in English of a single play of Goethe or Lessing; of Schiller only *Mary Stuart*. For a brief period in the nineteen-twenties German Expressionist plays were produced all over the world—such works as Toller's *Man and the Masses* or Kaiser's *Gas*; and they exercised a considerable influence on English and American playwrights and directors. But the classics of the German theatre have never flourished abroad. Is there something untranslatable in the German spirit? Or is it just that no good enough translation has yet appeared?

The French classics too have had but a poor showing in English. I think we are just beginning, as our stage gradually releases itself from the fetters of naturalism, to find a new sympathy with the spirit and theatrical form of Molière. On the other hand, I have read ten translations of Racine—careful, thoughtful, tasteful work—but none of them begin, in my opinion, to be actable. Most of them convert the Alexandrine verses of Racine into the rhythm of Shakespearian blank verse—to English ears far more natural. I wonder if this is wise? It certainly achieves a more familiar effect; it is certainly in this rhythm easier to find an English equivalent which is very close to the literal meaning of the original. But it is an altogether different music. I suspect that Racine is not well served by being rendered as a road-company Shakespeare. On the other hand, English Alexandrines are extraordinarily hard to write. We still await a translation not just of workmanlike skill and scholarly taste, but of genius, blazing with tragic fire. Until it is made, published, and, above all, gloriously acted, Racine must remain for the English-speaking public no more than a name in the textbooks, one of those fearsome bores, through whose work you plough because it is "on the syllabus."

This series will justify its existence if, here and there, a new translation enables a reader to find something more lively, more sympathetic in a play than existed there before; if the characters of Chekhov or of Gogol emerge first as human creatures and only second as Russians; if life in nineteenth-century Norway or seventeenth-century Germany is still recognizably life. Of course we do not hope that in exterior trappings any more than in processes of thought and feeling this "life" in foreign classics should exactly resemble our own lives. The life of a great work of art is necessarily larger, more high-colored, at once more orderly and more disturbed than our own little everyday existence. But a resemblance must be apparent. We must see that King Lear is, in a sense, everyone's father, just as Hamlet is Everyman. A good translation must reveal the universality of a great play without losing its individuality of time and place and character.

Since drama is primarily the raw material for dramatic performance and only secondarily, and incidentally, literature, each volume in this series will have a brief introduction by a theatrical director. The purpose of this is to help readers to think of the play in terms of an imagined performance; to try to persuade them to use the eyes and ears of imagination rather than just their minds. I am sure that no director will expect every reader to agree fully with all the ideas which he puts forward. But it is our hope that the mere fact of disagreement may stimulate readers to imagine more vividly for themselves and to remember that the printed text of a play bears to a performance the same relation as does the printed score of a symphony to the sound of an orchestra in the concert hall.

CHEKHOV AND THE CHERRY ORCHARD

BY LEONID KIPNIS

ANTON CHEKHOV was born January 17, 1860, in Taganrog, near Crimea. He died on July 2, 1904, in Badenweiler, Germany.

The earliest productions of Chekhov's plays had so little success that he was repeatedly discouraged from continuing his writing in this form. Still, the attraction to the theatre was so great that he kept returning—almost with trepidation, always with great inner suffering. In 1896 the first performance of Chekhov's *The Sea Gull* was a total failure. October 1898 saw the debut of the Moscow Art Theatre, and it, according to Vladimir Nemirovich-Danchenko (cofounder with Konstantin Stanislavsky of the theatre), was almost immediately "on the verge of complete collapse." Two months later, on December 17, 1898, the Moscow Art Theatre presented *The Sea Gull*—and it had instant success. From that moment on, these "failures," Chekhov and the Moscow Art Theatre, were inseparable.

Directly after the opening of *The Three Sisters* early in 1901 Stanislavsky, Nemirovich-Danchenko, and the other members of the theatre company began to press Chekhov for a new play. Partly because of ill health, which forced him to divide his time between Moscow and the warmer climate of Yalta in the Crimea, Chekhov was slow not only in beginning to write but even in conceiving this new play. March and April of 1901 still found him saying to friends: "My next play will most certainly be funny, very funny, at least in conception." "An enormous desire comes sometimes upon me to write . . . a vaudeville or a comedy . . . And I will write it if nothing comes in between." From then on, however, he became totally preoccupied with his new play, if not always actually working on it.

Slowly, character by character, scene by scene, the piece organically grew, though often it was physically scattered among small bits of paper. The final script appeared only after numerous interruptions—illness, traveling, short-story writing, all of which resulted in changes in the work itself. Yet, judging by the original notes, diaries, and letters concerning the play, the diversions were beneficial. (The excerpts from Chekhov's letters at the end of this volume trace the play's development.)

Many of the play's characters were composites of people he had met, brought together into new life by Chekhov's sensibility. How well he knew the people on the dying estates of his period, and the prototype of "the new breed," men like Lopahin! Certainly, he had no difficulty drawing the character of Trofimov from his memory of his own youth and from his constant observation of students. But all of his characters underwent continual change—sometimes so radical as to influence the whole play. For example, originally Ranevskaya was imagined as an old woman, too old to be played by Chekhov's actress-wife, Olga Knipper, who was finally to create the role. (Chekhov originally suggested she take the part of Varya.)

At last, instead of the boisterous comedy, the original "vaudeville" that Chekhov had wanted to write, *The Cherry Orchard* emerged. By September 26, 1903, the play was finished.

Rehearsals were a torture for the author, whose health at the time was steadily failing. While Chekhov had always seen his play as a comedy, with many light and gay scenes, Stanislavsky viewed it differently. "This is not a comedy, this is a tragedy," Stanislavsky wrote Chekhov; he called *The Cherry Orchard* a stark drama of Russian life. Chekhov was deeply disturbed by this disagreement over interpretation, yet he continued working on revisions and changes even after the play opened, on his birthday, January 17, 1904.

Although the critics were divided in their appraisal, the opening of *The Cherry Orchard* was a great theatrical event and the play was almost immediately presented in most of the important provincial cities in Russia. Only a short time elapsed before it received recognition abroad.

The original Moscow Art Theatre production was jointly directed by Stanislavsky and Nemirovich-Danchenko, with sets by Simoff. In 1958 Stavizin directed a "new" production with sets by Silitch. The changes were almost imperceptible, the most visible being slight ones in the second act sets and in the costumes, which stayed, however, in the epoch of the original. (In 1934 R. Simonoff's Theatre-Studio had attempted a completely revolutionized production of *The Cherry Orchard,* in which Ranevskaya was played as a courtesan and Yasha as a lover. This production was short-lived.) What is most amazing is that the acting in the Moscow Art Theatre presentation of the play remains, for the most part, unchanged. This is true to such a degree that words or expressions, differing from the published text, which crept into the original production (with Chekhov's approval) are still used.

A measure of the continuing popularity of the play in Russia is the fact that the Moscow Art Theatre alone has given more than 1,400 performances. The play has also been widely produced outside Russia: in Germany, Austria, England, France, Czechoslovakia, Turkey, China, Japan, even Iceland. In the United States hardly a season goes by without a professional production. (As a historical footnote, one might mention that there was a Broadway production of the play which transformed the cherry orchard into wisteria trees.)

Chekhov is now the only playwright of the turn of the century whose works are constantly performed all over the world. And no other play of his has met with the critical and popular acclaim of *The Cherry Orchard.* It shows Chekhov at his most mature, with a wonderful mixture of realism and irony. Russian as the play is, it is also international and therefore understood and accepted everywhere.

A DIRECTOR'S VIEW OF THE CHERRY ORCHARD

BY TYRONE GUTHRIE

LIKE ANY OTHER great play, in which the characters are more than superficially observed, *The Cherry Orchard* can be interpreted in many different ways.

At the first production in Moscow, as Leonid Kipnis has noted in the preceding pages, there was some difference of opinion between the author and the directors, Stanislavsky and Nemirovich-Danchenko. Chekhov faulted their interpretation for being too "tragic" and insisted that what he had written was a comedy.

It is rather too easy to argue that an author must know better than anyone else how his work ought to be interpreted. Is it not more true that the author must know best about the work which he *meant* to write, and which he *hopes* he has written? But what an author hopes that he means and what he actually expresses are not always quite the same thing.

Stanislavsky and Nemirovich-Danchenko were highly intelligent and talented men; also they had far more theatrical experience than Chekhov. Therefore they were surely entitled to their view of what the script meant—to them; and, as directors of the production, were not only entitled, but bound, to interpret it in their way. No doubt they will have been very much influenced by the author's disagreement, and will have made many changes, often against their better judgment; but, without their being able to help it, the interpretation will have, in general, been what *they* made of the script.

This possible divergence of view between creator and interpreter is not confined to playwrights and directors. An analogous divergence is constantly arising between composers and conductors. And there is a less precise, but still close, analogy concerning the divergence between what a painter or sculptor tries to express and what is made of his work by the critics and the public. Or again, take a novel: is it what the author meant to write and believes he has written? Or is it the impression which the novel makes upon each individual reader? In that case *David Copperfield,* for instance, means one thing to me, another to you; and neither of our impressions may be very close to Dickens' intention. Or is the essence of a work of art, perhaps, to be sought in a kind of amalgam of impressions—the impressions of every reader "processed" into the Average Viewpoint, as colorless, featureless, and deadly as that dismal abstraction: The Average Man.

Before we decide too glibly that the meaning of a complex work of art can be finally determined to be so-and-so, and therefore before we condemn those interpreters who may venture to "improve" upon the conscious intention of the creator—before doing this, let us consider what widely different interpretations may be put upon the very simplest sentence: "The cat sat on the mat" means one thing to a cat-lover in Bukhara; quite another to a cat-hater with a fluff allergy.

There is every reason to believe that the original production of *The Cherry Orchard,* despite the disagreements with the author, was a remarkably fine one. It may be suspected that with its directors' particular background, and especially with Stanislavsky playing Gaev, it may have leaned a little toward sentimentality about the dispossessed owners of the estate.

After the Bolshevik revolution—that is twelve years later—the balance, so I have heard, swung the other way: Trofimov became the central character. He became a symbol of ardent, idealistic youth, in revolt against decadent aristocracy, personified by Ranevskaya and her family, and against bourgeois materialism, personified by Lopahin.

This interpretation seems, if it ever really existed, to have been abandoned. In the Moscow Art Theatre's production which was seen in New York in February 1965, Trofimov was not accorded undue prominence. The actor looked suitably seedy and unprepossessing, and all the rodomontade about Progress was absolutely not delivered as a clarion call to revolution, not even as a serious prophecy about a Soviet millennium. Equally, neither Ranevskaya nor Gaev was sentimentalized, though neither performance was, in my opinion, a portrait which accorded too well with the evidence of the text. The portrayal of Lopahin, on the other hand, would, I believe, have been very acceptable to Chekhov. The text indicates that Lopahin is a sensitive and intelligent man; Trofimov says: "You have the hands of an artist and the feelings of an artist." Furthermore, Chekhov, in one of his letters, makes it clear that the part is not to be played as a coarse and vulgar upstart. The actor in the Moscow Art Theatre production looked extremely handsome, was far better dressed than anyone else, and only at the climax of the third act behaved in at all a vulgar or rough way, and then only momentarily and not in an obvious or overemphatic style.

I guess it was naive of me to be surprised and a little disillusioned to find that this theatre, together with the Abbey Theatre in Dublin, had grown old-fashioned. Sixty years ago these two theatres were far ahead of their time. Their writers, directors, and actors were exploring new territory, discovering new ways which seemed the more touching and thrilling because they were so simple, so unartificial. But neither the Moscow Art Theatre nor the Abbey seems to have been able to maintain a place in the theatre's vanguard. Both seem to be, temporarily no doubt, floating in the stagnant pond of a once successful style, which has long since been copycatted, developed, elaborated, and vulgarized by brisker, more commercial people; until now the once lively style seems uninteresting, unmoving, stale. No doubt life will come back to these two noble institutions which have so greatly influenced us all. Meantime it was sad to see a play so minutely, intimately, and imaginatively naturalistic presented by this theatre, which was the cradle and nurse of such naturalism, in what was, in my opinion, not just an old-fashioned, but an unimaginative and even unnatural style.

Actors took center stage for Big Moments; furniture was set in quite artificial and old-fashioned arrangements, with chairs and sofas conveniently placed so that actors could sink into them effectively and obviously, rather than naturally. In general, the rhythms and patterns of movement were uninteresting and uninventive. The scenery was poor too; however, most of the shortcomings on the visual side should probably be attributed to the difficulties inseparable from touring. But I had been hearing for years of the extraordinary verisimilitude which through scenery, lighting, and offstage sound effects so marvelously reinforced the actors of this company. Therefore it was rather a shock to find things as they were.

What was immensely impressive, however, was the solid professional strength of the company. One may not have agreed with all the casting, or admired without qualification all the performers, but there could be no gainsaying the general impression that a group of intelligent, highly trained people knew just what they were trying to do and why. There was a solid sense of unified endeavor, which had nothing whatever to do with politics, but was concerned entirely with artistic purpose. This is the result partly of an economic security which membership in a permanent repertory company gives to the actors; partly of a tradition, and a solidarity of companionship in, and loyalty to, an institution, which the short-term policies and flimsy managerial structures of our Western theatre simply do not engender.

To present Chekhov the Western theatre must make some translation in manner as well as in language. Just as the Russian language is rather more emotional and effusive than our own, so is Russian acting. Again and again Chekhov's stage directions read "through tears" or "weeping," on occasions when no doubt a Russian man or woman would act so, but when we of the Western world would maintain far stiffer upper lips. My belief is that we should not try to force ourselves into the extreme expressions of grief and joy which come quite easily and naturally to Slavs; and that, keyed down to our more restrained behavior, the play can be no less poignant, and its meaning no less clear.

The Chekhov productions of the Minnesota Theatre Company have been given on an open stage—a platform surrounded on three sides by the audience—where there can really be no attempt at dramatic illusion. *Uncle Vanya* was produced at Chichester, by Sir Laurence Olivier and the British National Theatre, in similar circumstances and with outstanding success.

Something is lost on the open stage; and something is gained. There is a loss of dramatic illusion. But ought we to demand of drama that it create illusion? It is my view that no one beyond the mental age of nine believes that what is happening on the stage is "really" happening. You know perfectly well that you are sitting in a theatre watching somebody on a stage pretending to be Hamlet. You do not believe yourself really to be in Elsinore, any more than, when you are reading a novel, you believe that you are present with Pierre Bezukhov at the battle of Borodino, or with Alice at the Red Queen's croquet party. It is true that, if a novel is good enough, you can be completely lost, totally transported, taken, as they say, out of yourself into an imaginary world. This happens too when a theatrical experience is good enough. But then it also happens at a good concert; with music, however, there is no question of illusion. You are rapt, transported, rendered oblivious of time, place, and all mundane considerations. But this is not the same thing as being rendered incapable of distinguishing between plain fact and palpable fiction.

Therefore I do not feel that a reduction of dramatic illusion is fatal to Chekhov. There may, however, on an open stage be loss of "atmosphere," especially in the matters of scenery and lighting. This is partly counterbalanced by a gain in intimacy, since the open stage permits the audience to be physically nearer to the actors; and a gain in flexibility and naturalness of choreography. Above all, on an open stage the exterior scenes—and Chekhov sets many of his scenes out of doors—can be presented with just the same degree of realism, or unrealism, as the indoor scenes. In a proscenium theatre it is hard, if not impossible, to avoid a jolting change of convention, since interiors can be rendered with elaborate realistic accuracy, whereas the exterior scenes can be no more than highly stylized, painted landscapes, "masked" by "wings," with "borders" overhead, which, however beautifully painted, however skillfully lit, are still not very like whatever they are pretending to be.

English productions of *The Cherry Orchard* have tended to present Ranevskaya and Gaev rather more sentimentally than was, I believe, the author's intention. The pathos of the dispossessed upper classes struck sympathetic chords in an epoch when taxation was making the maintenance of large old country-houses and estates increasingly difficult, and when a universally hideous "suburban sprawl" rightly tended to discredit Lopahin's projected housing development. In London in 1963 Michel Saint-Denis directed a revival which deliberately aimed to avoid sentiment about the poor, dear upper classes. It was not received with unmixed praise. Dramatic critics cling with touching faithfulness to theatrical stereotypes. It will be many a year before critics abandon the idea that this is a sad play about a charming, gracious heroine, who suffers undeserved misfortune at the hands of an ungrateful and insensitive vulgarian.

This translation has been made for a production by the Minnesota Theatre Company. There exist already a number of translations; but the American ones seemed to us a little too vernacular; they smacked too obviously of the mid-twentieth century and of an urban, slightly inelegant milieu. Hubert Butler's translation, made for the Old Vic production of 1933, is already a little dated. John Gielgud did an excellent version in the nineteen-fifties, but it seemed for our purpose a little too British in its turns of phrase.

We are aware that, while a great masterpiece is hardly affected at all by the passage of time, its translations into other languages do "date" extremely soon. One tries hard to avoid words and turns of phrase which are associated with a particular time or place; but it is a vain attempt. Without our being aware of it, we express ourselves and our environment, and this quickly becomes jarring and irrelevant. A great translation may acquire validity in its own right—for example, the Schlegel-Tieck versions of Shakespeare in German, or those of Zhukovski or Pasternak in Russian. A very good translation may be acceptable for a generation or two. Most seem utterly "dated" after no more than ten years; one must return again and again to the original text and interpret it anew.

The Play

CHARACTERS

MADAME RANEVSKAYA, Lyubov Andreyevna, the owner of the cherry orchard

ANYA, her daughter, aged about eighteen

VARYA, her adopted daughter, somewhat older

GAEV, Leonid Andreyevich, Madame Ranevskaya's brother

LOPAHIN, Yermolai Alexeyevich, a merchant

TROFIMOV, Pyotr Sergeyevich, a student

SIMEONOFF-PISHCHIK, owner of a neighboring estate

CHARLOTTA IVANOVNA, a governess

YEPIHODOV, a clerk on Madame Ranevskaya's estate

DUNYASHA, a maid

FIRS, a servant, age eighty-seven

YASHA, a young servant

A passer-by

Station master

A post office employee

Guests and servants

The action of the play takes place in Russia at the beginning of this century on Madame Ranevskaya's estate.

ACT ONE

A room which is still called the nursery. One of the doors leads into Anya's room. It is dawn: the sun will be up soon. It is May, the cherry trees are in flower, but it is cold in the garden, with early morning frost. All windows are closed.

Enter DUNYASHA *with a candle and* LOPAHIN *with a book.*

LOPAHIN

The train's in, thank God. What time is it?

DUNYASHA

Almost four o'clock. (*Blows out candle*) It's light already.

LOPAHIN

I wonder how late the train is. Two hours, anyway. (*Yawns and stretches*) I'm a great one! I've made a fool of myself! I came here specially to meet them at the station and fell asleep, if you please, in my chair. Idiotic . . . you might have wakened me up.

DUNYASHA

I thought you'd gone away. Listen! They're coming!

LOPAHIN

(*listens*) No . . . there's the luggage and that to see to . . . (*Pause*) Lyubov Andreyevna's been abroad for five years. What will she be like now? . . . She's a fine person—an easy, simple person! I remember when I was a boy about fifteen, my father, God rest him, he kept a store in the village then, cracked me in the face with his fist, made my nose bleed . . . We'd come here, the pair of us, for some reason or other. He'd had a few drinks. Lyubov Andreyevna, I remember it as if it was yesterday, she was just a girl, skinny, she brought me to the washstand in this very room, the nursery. "Don't cry, little boy," she said. "You'll be yourself again by your wedding day." (*Pause*) "Little boy." It's true, my father just lived in the village and look at me now, white waistcoat, brown shoes—talk about a pig in clover . . . I'm rich, now, lots of money, but when you come to think of it, when you get right down to things, I'm just my father's son. (*Fluttering the pages of the book*) Here I've been reading this and didn't take in a thing. I read it and fell asleep. (*Pause*)

DUNYASHA

The dogs have been awake all night. They can feel their people are coming home.

LOPAHIN

What is it, Dunyasha? You are so . . .

DUNYASHA

I'm trembling. I believe I'm going to faint.

LOPAHIN

You act so refined, Dunyasha. Got up like a young lady too. And look at your hair. It's all wrong, you know. You're forgetting who you are.

YEPIHODOV *comes in with a bunch of flowers; he is in his Sunday best, with shiny boots which squeak loudly. As he comes in he drops the flowers.*

YEPIHODOV

(*picking up the flowers*) The gardener sent these in. Put them in the dining room, he says. Here. (*Gives the flowers to* DUNYASHA)

LOPAHIN

(*to* DUNYASHA) And bring me some kvass.

DUNYASHA

Very well. (DUNYASHA *goes*)

YEPIHODOV

A frost this morning—three degrees, and the cherries all in flower. I can't say I approve of our climate (*sighs*). I really can't. Our climate is really rather unhelpful, if one is to be strictly accurate! And look, Yermolai Alexeyevich, if you'll please excuse my saying so: I bought myself a pair of boots the day before yesterday and I venture to assure you that they squeak in a totally impossible manner. What should I grease them with?

LOPAHIN

That's enough. That'll do.

YEPIHODOV

Each and every day something unlucky happens to me. But I don't complain. I am accustomed to it. I even smile at it.

DUNYASHA *comes in and gives the kvass to* LOPAHIN.

YEPIHODOV

Well, I'll be off. (*Bumps against a chair which falls*) There! (*Triumphantly*) What did I tell you? Misfortunes never come singly. (YEPIHODOV *goes*)

DUNYASHA

Yermolai Alexeyevich, I want to tell you something: Yepihodov has proposed to me.

LOPAHIN

Mm?

DUNYASHA

I really don't know . . . He's all right. But sometimes he starts talking and you don't really understand a thing. It's beautiful, of course, and full of feeling—only you can't understand a thing. I sort of like him. He's wild for me. He's an unlucky fellow. Each and every day some misfortune happens to him. Everyone here calls him "Never come singly."

LOPAHIN

(*listening*) Listen! There they are!

DUNYASHA

They're here! What's the matter with me? I'm trembling!

LOPAHIN

They're really here! Let's go and meet them. Will she recognize me—it's been five years.

DUNYASHA

(*agitated*) I shall faint. I know I shall.

Carriages are heard approaching. LOPAHIN *and* DUNYASHA *go out hurriedly. The stage is empty. Then the neighboring rooms begin to be alive, noisy.* FIRS, *leaning on a cane, hurriedly crosses the stage. He's been to meet* MADAME RANEVSKAYA *and still wears his old livery and top hat. He speaks to himself but one can't understand a word. The noise backstage is intensified. A voice:* "Let's come in here . . ." MADAME RANEVSKAYA, ANYA, *and* CHARLOTTA IVANOVNA, *with a dog on a chain, come in. All are dressed for travel.*

VARYA *is in an overcoat and shawl.* GAEV, SIMEONOFF-PISHCHIK, LOPAHIN, DUNYASHA *with a bundle and parasol, servants with pieces of luggage—all go through.*

ANYA

Let's come through here. You remember this room, mamma?

RANEVSKAYA

(*through happy tears*) The nursery!

VARYA

Oh it's cold! My hands are numb. (*To* RANEVSKAYA) Your rooms are just as they were, darling mamma, the white one and the lilac.

RANEVSKAYA

The nursery, my own dear nursery—what a sweet old room it is! . . . I used to sleep here when I was little . . . and now it's as if I were little again . . . (*Kisses* GAEV, VARYA, *then her brother again*) And Varya is just the same as ever—like a nun. And of course I knew Dunyasha too. (*Kisses* DUNYASHA)

GAEV

The train was two hours late. What about that? What kind of organization is that?

CHARLOTTA

(*to* PISHCHIK) My dog eats nuts.

PISHCHIK

(*astonished*) Just fancy that!

Everybody goes out except ANYA *and* DUNYASHA.

DUNYASHA

We've been waiting and waiting . . . (*Takes off* ANYA's *coat and hat*)

ANYA

What a journey! I haven't slept for four nights. Now I'm perishing.

DUNYASHA

You went away in Lent—there was snow then and frost, and now . . . Oh my dearest (*laughs, kisses her*). I've been waiting and waiting for you, my love, my angel . . . now I'll tell you at once. I can't wait another minute . . .

ANYA

(*without enthusiasm*) Not again . . .

DUNYASHA

After Holy Week Yepihodov proposed to me.

ANYA

It's always the same with you . . . (*Tidying her hair*) I've lost all my hairpins. (*She is very tired; she sways on her feet*)

DUNYASHA

I don't know what to think, really I don't. He loves me—oh so very much.

ANYA

(*looks at the door of her room*) My room. My windows. It's as if I'd never been away. I'm home. Tomorrow morning I'll get up and run out into the garden. Oh if I could only sleep! I didn't sleep on the journey at all. I was so worried.

DUNYASHA

Do you know who turned up the day before yesterday? Trofimov.

ANYA

(*joyfully*) Petya!

DUNYASHA

He's sleeping in the bathhouse. Living there actually. I don't want to be a nuisance, he says. (*Looking at her watch*) I ought to wake him up but your sister Varya told me not to. Don't wake him up, she said.

VARYA *comes in, a bunch of keys at her waist.*

VARYA

Dunyasha. Coffee. Quick . . . darling mamma wants her coffee.

DUNYASHA

This very minute. (DUNYASHA *goes*)

VARYA

Thank God you're all here! You're home again (*lovingly*). My little darling has come home! My lovely little angel has come home.

ANYA

It's been awful.

VARYA

I can imagine!

ANYA

I left in Lent. It was cold then. Charlotta never stopped talking, doing her tricks. Why did you have to hang Charlotta round my neck?

VARYA

But, darling, you could not travel all alone. At seventeen!

ANYA

We got to Paris; it was cold there and snowy. My French is horrible. There was mamma way up on the fifth floor. When I got there the room was full of the oddest people, Frenchmen and ladies, an old priest with a book. They were all smoking. It was all so . . . Suddenly I felt terribly sorry for mamma. I felt so sorry for her, I hugged her and couldn't let her go. And mamma was at her very nicest and sweetest. She cried.

VARYA

(*weeping*) Don't tell me. Don't tell me.

ANYA

She had already sold the villa on the Riviera. She hadn't anything left. And I hadn't anything left either—not a thing. We only just managed to get there. And mamma doesn't realize! When we dine in a station restaurant she insists upon the most expensive things and leaves far too large a tip. Charlotta's just the same. Yasha insists upon having the same things as we do. It's simply awful. You know Yasha's mamma's footman now. We've brought him back with us.

VARYA

Yes. I've seen him—nasty thing.

ANYA

Well now, tell me: has the interest been paid?

VARYA

How could it?

ANYA

Oh dear! Oh dear!

VARYA

In August they're going to sell the estate.

ANYA

Oh dear!

LOPAHIN

(*looking in at the door*) Baa!! (*He goes*)

VARYA

(*through tears*) That's what I'd like to do to him! (*Shakes her fist*)

ANYA

(*embracing* VARYA) Varya, has he asked you to marry him?

VARYA *shakes her head.*

ANYA

But he loves you . . . Why don't you talk it over like two sensible people? What are you waiting for?

VARYA

Do you know what I think? Nothing's going to come of it. He's so busy. He has no time for me. He doesn't even notice me. I can't bear even to see him, God help him . . . Everyone's talking about our marriage, everyone offers congratulations, but really and truly there's nothing in it. It's all like a dream . . . You've got a little brooch like a bee.

ANYA

(*sadly*) Mamma bought it. (*Goes toward her room speaking gaily, almost like a child*) And in Paris I went up in a balloon!

VARYA

My little darling has come home. My lovely little angel has come home.

DUNYASHA *comes in with the coffee tray.*

VARYA

(*near Anya's door*) All the time that I'm busy about the house, I keep on dreaming. If we could only marry you off to a rich man! What a weight it would take off my mind! Then I should set off as a pilgrim, first to Kiev . . .

to Moscow. I should wander on from one holy place to another. On and on, it would be heavenly.

ANYA

The birds are singing in the garden. What time is it?

VARYA

It must be nearly five. Time you went to sleep, darling . . . (*They go toward Anya's room*) Heavenly!

YASHA *comes in with a traveling rug and bag.*

YASHA

(*tiptoeing across the room*) May one go through here?

DUNYASHA

Yasha! I shouldn't have known you. How you've changed abroad!

YASHA

Hm! And who may you be?

DUNYASHA

When you went away I was only so high! I'm Dunyasha, Fyodor Kosoyedov's daughter. You don't remember!

YASHA

Hm! . . . A nice little piece.

YASHA *looks around and puts his arm around her: she screams, breaks a saucer.* YASHA *goes out quickly.*

VARYA

(*at door of Anya's room, vexed*) What is it?

DUNYASHA

(*nearly in tears*) I broke a saucer . . .

VARYA

Oh well, that's good luck.

ANYA

(*coming out of her room*) We should warn mamma that Petya's here.

VARYA

I told them he wasn't to be wakened.

ANYA

(*thoughtfully*) Six years since father died. A month later my brother Grisha was drowned in the river. Such a sweet little boy, he was only seven. Mamma simply couldn't bear it. She went away, she went right away (*shuddering*). If she only knew how well I understand her. (*Pause*) And Petya Trofimov was Grisha's tutor. Seeing him would bring it all back to her . . .

FIRS *comes in, in a jacket and white waistcoat.*

FIRS

(*at the coffee tray*) The mistress will have her coffee in here. (*Puts on white gloves*) Is the coffee ready? (*To* DUNYASHA, *vexed*) You! Where's the cream?

DUNYASHA

Oh my God . . . (*rushes out*)

FIRS

Ech! Silly young cuckoo! (*Mumbles to himself*)
They're home from Paris . . . The old master—he went to Paris once . . . It was horses then (*laughs*).

VARYA

What is it, Firs?

FIRS

At your service. (*Joyfully*) The mistress is home! I've lived to see it . . . now I can die (*weeps for joy*).

MADAME RANEVSKAYA, GAEV, *and* SIMEONOFF-PISHCHIK *come in.* SIMEONOFF-PISHCHIK *is in a peasant coat made of a very fine cloth and wide trousers tucked into the top of his boots.* GAEV'S *movements—both his arms and body—suggest a person playing billiards.*

RANEVSKAYA

How does it go? Let's see . . . One ball in the corner! And two in the middle.

GAEV

Cutting into the corner. Time was, sister, when you and I slept in this very room, and now—strange to relate, I'm fifty-one years old . . .

LOPAHIN

Yes. Time flies.

GAEV

What?

LOPAHIN

Time flies, I said.

GAEV

There's a smell of cheap scent.

ANYA

I'm going to sleep. Good night, mamma (*kisses her mother*).

RANEVSKAYA

You dear little thing (*kisses her hands*). Are you happy to be home? I still can't believe it.

ANYA

Good night, uncle.

GAEV

(*kisses her cheeks and hands*) God be with you, darling! You're the image of your mother! At her age, Lyuba, you were exactly like this child.

ANYA *shakes hands with* LOPAHIN *and* PISHCHIK, *goes out, and closes the door behind her.*

RANEVSKAYA

She's tired out.

PISHCHIK

I suppose it's been a long way.

VARYA

(*to* LOPAHIN *and* PISHCHIK) It's about five, gentlemen, time's up!

RANEVSKAYA

(*laughing*) The same old Varya (*hugs her*). I'll just finish my coffee, then we'll go. (FIRS *sets a cushion under her feet*) Thank you, my dear. I simply can't do without my coffee. I drink it day and night. Thank you, you dear old thing (*kisses* FIRS).

VARYA

I must go see whether they've brought in all your things. (*Goes out*)

RANEVSKAYA

Am I really sitting here? (*Laughs*) I could dance about and wave my arms. (*Hides her face in her hands*) Perhaps I am dreaming. God knows I love my home, I love it, I love it. I couldn't look out of the train; I was crying too much. (*Through tears*) But I must have my coffee just the same. Thank you, Firs. Thank you, you dear old thing. It's so good that you are still alive.

FIRS

The day before yesterday.

GAEV

Deaf as a post.

LOPAHIN

I've got to catch the train to Kharkov at six. Isn't it annoying? I wanted so much just to look at you and have a talk . . . You're as splendid as ever.

PISHCHIK

(*breathing heavily*) Even more so. Paris fashions. I'm knocked absolutely flat.

LOPAHIN

Your brother here is always saying what a coarse, money-grubbing fellow I am. Well, I don't care. Let him say what he likes. All I want is that you should trust me as you used to, that you should look at me in that wonderful, moving way of yours. God have mercy! My father was a serf of your father and your grandfather before him, but you—and no one but you—once did so much for me that I forgot the whole of that and I love you as if you were one of my own . . . more than one of my own.

RANEVSKAYA

I can't sit here another second. I really can't . . . (*Jumps up and walks about in great emotion*) I can't live through such happiness . . . Laugh at me if you like, I know I'm silly . . . My dear bookcase (*kisses bookcase*), my little table.

GAEV

Nurse died while you were away.

RANEVSKAYA

(*sits down and drinks coffee*) Yes, the Kingdom of Heaven be hers. You wrote me.

GAEV

Anatasyi is dead too. Petrushka Kosoy has left me—he works in town now, for the captain of police (*takes a box of sweets out of his pocket and begins to suck one*).

PISHCHIK

My daughter Dashenka . . . sends her love.

LOPAHIN

I've got something very pleasant to tell you, something nice. (*Looks at watch*) But I have to go now. No time to talk . . . Oh well, in a couple of words . . . You know that your whole estate including the cherry orchard is going to be sold to pay your debts. The sale is fixed for the twenty-second of August. But don't worry my dear, you needn't lose any sleep over it. There's a way out . . . Here's my plan: now listen. Your estate isn't more than fifteen miles from town and now the railroad runs quite near and if the cherry orchard and the land by the river were divided up into small lots and rented out for summer cottages, it would bring you in a very substantial annual income.

GAEV

Excuse me, but that's absolute rubbish!

RANEVSKAYA

I don't think I quite understand you, Yermolai Alexeyevich.

LOPAHIN

You should get at least twenty-five rubles an acre each year from the summer residents. And if you let it be known at once, I'll absolutely guarantee that you won't have a single empty lot, they'll all be taken up. In short, congratulations, the day is saved. It's a wonderful situation, a deep river. But of course it would have to be cleared up . . . all the old buildings would have to come down, naturally—this house too, which is no good for anything. The old cherry orchard would have to be cut down . . .

RANEVSKAYA

Cut down? My dear man, you don't know what you're talking about. If there's one thing in the whole province which is interesting, yes even remarkable, it's our cherry orchard.

LOPAHIN

The only remarkable thing about your orchard is that it's very large. The trees only bear cherries every other year and even so nobody buys them.

GAEV

Our cherry orchard is even mentioned in the *Encyclopedia.*

LOPAHIN

(*looking at his watch*) If we don't think of anything and don't come to any decision, then the cherry orchard and the whole estate will be put up for sale on the twenty-second of August. So make up your minds! There's no other way out, I assure you, no other way out at all.

FIRS

In the old days, forty—fifty years ago they used to dry the cherries, or soak them in brine, preserve them, make them into jam and sometimes . . .

GAEV

That'll do, Firs.

FIRS

And the dried cherries used to be sent by the wagon load to Moscow and Kharkov. There was money in those days! And the dried cherries were soft and juicy and sweet. They smelled delicious . . . In those days they knew the way to . . .

RANEVSKAYA

And why don't they know now?

FIRS

Forgotten. Nobody remembers anymore.

PISHCHIK

(*to* RANEVSKAYA) What's it like in Paris? Did you eat frogs?

RANEVSKAYA

I ate crocodiles.

PISHCHIK

Fancy that! . . .

LOPAHIN

Up till now there's been nobody in the country but gentry and peasants; but now summer residents have arrived upon the scene. All the cities, even quite small ones, are surrounded now by summer cottages. And it is safe to say that in twenty years these summer people will multiply incredibly. Right now they just drink tea on the porch but who knows when they won't start cultivating their little plots and then your cherry orchard will become a useful place, rich and glorious.

GAEV

(*shocked*) What rubbish!

VARYA

Mamma darling, two cables for you. (*Chooses a key and opens the old bookcase, which creaks*) Here they are.

RANEVSKAYA

From Paris (*tears them up*). I've finished with Paris.

GAEV

Do you know, Lyuba, how old this bookcase is? Last week I pulled out the bottom drawer and looked—the date has been burnt into it. This bookcase was made exactly a hundred years ago. Just think of that! There should have been a celebration for its centenary. It's only an inanimate object, but all the same it is a bookcase.

PISHCHIK

(*astonished*) A hundred years . . . just fancy that!

GAEV

Yes . . . it's a good old thing . . . (*Patting it*) My dear and most esteemed bookcase. Hail to thee who, for more than a hundred years hast kept us in mind of the high ideals of goodness and justice; in a hundred years thy silent call to fruitful work has never faltered, supporting (*through tears*) through all our generations the belief in a better future, inculcating in us the notion of virtue and of our duty as citizens.

Pause.

LOPAHIN

Yes . . .

RANEVSKAYA

Leonid, you haven't changed a bit.

GAEV

(*embarrassed*) Into right corner! Cannon off the cushion!

LOPAHIN

(*looking at watch*) Time's up. I must go.

YASHA

(*giving her medicine to* RANEVSKAYA) Will you take your pills now?

PISHCHIK

You shouldn't take stuff like that, my dear . . . Does you no harm and no good . . . Give them to me, adorable lady! (*Takes the pills, tips them into the palm of his hand, blows on them, puts them all into his mouth, and swallows them with a mouthful of kvass*) You see!

RANEVSKAYA

(*alarmed*) You are out of your mind!

PISHCHIK

I've taken all the pills.

LOPAHIN

Greedy guts.

All laugh.

FIRS

They were here one Easter and ate half a bucket of cucumbers . . . (*Mumbles*)

RANEVSKAYA

What's he talking about?

VARYA

He's been mumbling like that for three years. We've got used to it.

YASHA

It's a matter of age, actually.

CHARLOTTA IVANOVNA *comes in, in a white dress, very thin, tightly corseted with a lorgnette at her belt. She passes across.*

LOPAHIN

Forgive me, Charlotta Ivanovna, I didn't have a chance to ask how you were (*attempts to kiss her hand*).

CHARLOTTA

(*pulling her hand away*) If I let you kiss my hand, next thing you'll want to kiss my elbow, then my shoulder.

LOPAHIN

This isn't my lucky day! (*All laugh*) Charlotta Ivanovna, do one of your tricks!

RANEVSKAYA

Oh yes, Charlotta, do.

CHARLOTTA

I shan't. I want to go to sleep. (*Goes out*)

LOPAHIN

See you in three weeks (*kisses* RANEVSKAYA's *hand*). Farewell for now. Time's up. (*To* GAEV) Good-bye. (*Kisses* PISHCHIK) Good-bye. (*Shakes hands with* VARYA, *then* FIRS *and* YASHA) I wish I didn't have to go. (*To* RANEVSKAYA) Now think it over, about the summer cottages, and if you decide to sell, let me know. I'll get you a loan of fifty thousand. Now mind and think it over carefully.

VARYA

(*angrily*) Oh do go.

LOPAHIN

Going, going. (*He goes*)

GAEV

Scum! Oh excuse me . . . Varya is going to marry him. He's Varya's "intended."

VARYA

Now, uncle dear, don't talk like that.

RANEVSKAYA

Well but, Varya, I should be very glad. He's a decent creature.

PISHCHIK

If we're going to be strictly truthful, it's an extremely worthy creature . . . and my Dashenka . . . she says . . . lots of things (*snores but wakes up again at once*). But all the same, adorable lady, just lend me two hundred and forty rubles . . . the interest on my mortgage is due tomorrow.

VARYA

(*in a panic*) We don't have it! We don't have it!

RANEVSKAYA

As a matter of fact I simply haven't a thing.

PISHCHIK

It'll turn up (*laughs*). I never give up hope. For instance, I thought that I was utterly ruined, when lo and behold they put the railroad right across my land and . . . paid me for it. Something'll turn up, if not today, tomorrow . . . Dashenka will win two hundred thousand . . . she has a ticket in the lottery.

RANEVSKAYA

Well, we've finished our coffee; let's retire, friends.

FIRS

(*brushes at* GAEV'*s coat; as to a child*) You're in the wrong trousers again! What shall I do with you!

VARYA

(*in a low tone*) Anya's asleep. (*Softly opens the window*) The sun is up. It isn't cold anymore . . . Look, mamma darling. Isn't it beautiful? So fresh. The birds are singing.

GAEV

(*opening another window*) The whole orchard is white. You haven't forgotten it, Lyuba? Look down there—between the trees—straight, straight as far as the eye can see. On moonlight nights it shines like a ribbon of silver. Do you remember? You haven't forgotten?

RANEVSKAYA

(*looks out of the window*) Oh my childhood! My innocence! I used to sleep in this very room. I looked out from here over the orchard. Happiness woke with me each morning. And here it is. The same as ever. (*Laughs with joy*) All, all white! Oh my orchard! After the dark, wild autumn and the cold winter you are young again, full of joy; God's heavenly angels haven't forsaken you . . . Oh if I could only cast off the millstone which is weighing me down; if I could only forget my past . . .

GAEV

Yes. And the orchard's going to be sold to pay our debts. Strange as that may seem!

RANEVSKAYA

Oh look! Mamma—walking in the orchard in a white dress. (*Laughs happily*) There she is!

GAEV

Where?

VARYA

Oh no, no!

RANEVSKAYA

There's no one there! I was just imagining it. Over there, just beside the arbor, there's a white tree leaning over like a little bent woman . . . (TROFIMOV *comes in, in an old student uniform and glasses*) What a heavenly orchard. Masses of white flowers, blue sky . . .

TROFIMOV

Lyubov Andreyevna (*she looks at him*) I've just looked in to see you. I'll go again at once. (*Fervently kisses her hand*) They told me to wait till tomorrow. But I just couldn't . . .

RANEVSKAYA *looks at him at a loss.*

VARYA

(*moved*) It's Petya Trofimov.

TROFIMOV

Petya Trofimov. I used to be your Grisha's tutor. Do I look so different?

RANEVSKAYA *embraces him and weeps.*

GAEV

(*embarrassed*) That'll do, Lyuba, that'll do.

VARYA

(*crying*) I told you, Petya, you should have waited.

RANEVSKAYA

My Grisha . . . my boy . . . Grisha . . . my son . . .

VARYA

It was God's will, mamma darling. What can we do?

TROFIMOV

(*gently*) Don't cry. Don't cry . . .

RANEVSKAYA

(*crying*) The boy is lost. Drowned. Why? Why? Will somebody please tell me why? (*More quietly*) Anya's asleep there, and here I am making all this noise . . . and you, Petya, you look so plain. Why do you look so old?

TROFIMOV

A woman on the train called me a seedy-looking gent.

RANEVSKAYA

You were just a boy then, a nice little student. And now look at you! Your hair's getting thin, and glasses! And is it true that you're still a student? (*She goes to the door*)

TROFIMOV

It looks as if I should be a perennial student.

RANEVSKAYA

(*kisses her brother, then* VARYA) Well, go to sleep . . . and you're old too, Leonid.

PISHCHIK

(*following her*) All right. So we have to go to sleep . . . oh, my gout! . . . I'll stay, if you'll keep me . . . and tomorrow morning, my dear Lyubov Andreyevna, I've just got to have that two hundred and forty.

GAEV

Always the same old story.

PISHCHIK

Two hundred and forty. It's the interest on my mortgage.

RANEVSKAYA

But, my dear man, I haven't any money.

PISHCHIK

I'll pay it back, my dear . . . it's such an insignificant amount.

RANEVSKAYA

Oh very well. Leonid will give it to you . . . Give it to him, Leonid.

GAEV

(*ironically*) Of course.

RANEVSKAYA

What else can we do? Give it to him . . . he needs it. He'll pay it back.

RANEVSKAYA, PISHCHIK, *and* TROFIMOV *go out.* VARYA, GAEV, *and* YASHA *remain.*

GAEV

Sister still throws her money about. (*To* YASHA) Get out of the way, my man, you smell of tobacco.

YASHA

(*with a grin*) And you, Leonid Andreyevich, you're just the same as ever.

GAEV

What's that? (*To* VARYA) What did he say?

VARYA

(*to* YASHA) Your mother's come up from the village. She's been waiting in the servants' quarters since yesterday. She wants to see you.

YASHA

(*grimacing*) Oh . . .

VARYA

You ought to be ashamed of yourself.

YASHA

Well, why should I care? She could have come tomorrow. (*Goes*)

VARYA

Darling mamma is just the same as ever. She hasn't changed a bit. If she could, she'd give away everything she has.

GAEV

Yes . . . (*Pause*) When all kinds of cures are suggested for a disease, it means that the disease is incurable. Here have I been racking my brains in every possible way, in every possible way, which means that I've thought of nothing. It would be a nice thing if someone left us a fortune; it would be nice to marry Anya off to a very rich man. It would be good if I went to Yaroslav and tried my luck with my aunt, the countess—she's as rich as ever she can be.

VARYA

(*crying*) If only God would help us.

GAEV

Don't blubber! The aunt is very rich but she doesn't like us. In the first place my sister married a lawyer, not a nobleman (ANYA *is at the door of her room*); she didn't marry a nobleman and one couldn't say that her behavior was entirely virtuous; she's a kind good soul, I love her very much, but no matter what allowances one tries to make, one has to admit that there's something, well—sort of loose about her.

VARYA

Ssh! (*Whispering*) Anya at the door.

GAEV

What? (*Pause*) Odd thing! I've got something in my right eye. I can't see properly. And on Thursday when I was in the District Court . . .

ANYA *comes in.*

VARYA

Why aren't you asleep, Anya?

ANYA

I can't sleep.

GAEV

My baby (*kisses her face and hands*). My child—you're not my niece, you're my angel. You're everything in the world to me. Believe me, believe me.

ANYA

I believe you, uncle dear. Everybody loves you, respects you . . . but uncle dear, you must not talk so much. You simply must hold your tongue. What were you saying about my mother—your sister? Why did you say it?

GAEV

I know. I know. (*Covers his face with* ANYA's *hand*) It's really horrible! Oh my God! My God! Help me! And today I made a speech to the bookcase . . . So silly . . . It was only when I'd finished that I realized how silly it was.

VARYA

It's true, uncle dear, you really must not talk so much. Just don't talk so much.

ANYA

If only you wouldn't talk so much it would be so much better for you.

GAEV

I'll hold my tongue (*kisses* VARYA's *and* ANYA's *hands*), I really will. But this is business. On Thursday I was in the District Court, a group of us started chatting about this and that, and it seems as if it might be possible to arrange a loan which would take care of the bank interest.

VARYA

If only God would help us!

GAEV

I'll go there on Tuesday and we'll speak about it again. (*To* VARYA) Don't blubber. (*To* ANYA) Your mother will speak to Lopahin; he certainly won't refuse her . . . and as for you—after you're rested—you'll go to Yaroslav to your great-aunt, the countess. And so we'll attack it from three sides at once and we can't miss the target. (*Puts a candy in his mouth*) I swear by my happiness. Here's my hand. Call me a cheat, call me a rogue, if I let the sale go through! I swear it with all my heart and soul.

ANYA

(*happy and relieved*) Uncle, how good you are! And how clever! (*Embraces him*) What a relief! What a wonderful relief!

FIRS *comes in.*

FIRS

(*reproachfully*) Leonid Andreyevich, have you no fear of God! When are you going to bed?

GAEV

Coming, coming. You go, Firs. Tonight I'll undress myself! Night night, children . . . bed now . . . plans tomorrow (*kisses them*). I'm a man of the eighties . . . some people have no use for the eighties, but I'm here to say that in my time I've got into plenty of trouble for my beliefs. It isn't for nothing that your peasant loves me. One has to know one's peasant! One has to know how to . . .

ANYA

Uncle, you're off again.

VARYA

Uncle dear, hold your tongue.

FIRS

(*angrily*) Leonid Andreyevich!

GAEV

Coming. Coming . . .

He goes, followed by FIRS.

ANYA

I feel so relieved. I feel better about it all. I don't want to go to Yaroslav. I don't like my great-aunt. But still I feel better about it all. Thanks to uncle. (*Sits down*)

VARYA

Time to go to sleep. I'm going. Anya, while you were away something rather unpleasant happened. As you know there are only old people in what used to be the servants' quarters: Yefimka, Polya, Evstigney, oh, and Karp too. They began to let all sorts of odd people in for the night—I didn't say a word, I pretended not to notice. But then I hear a rumor that I've given orders to feed them nothing but dried peas—out of stinginess, if you please . . . Well it all comes from Evstigney. Very well, I think to myself. If that's the case, I think, just you wait. I send for Evstigney. "Evstigney," I said (*yawns*), "how can you be such an idiot . . . (*Looks at* ANYA) Anitchka! (*Pause*) She's asleep. (*Takes her by the arm*) Let's go to bed. Come (*takes her*). My own darling has fallen asleep. Come. (*They go*)

Far off in the garden a shepherd plays a reed pipe. TROFIMOV *crosses the stage, sees* VARYA *and* ANYA *and stops.*

VARYA

Tss! She's asleep . . . asleep. Come darling.

ANYA

(*half asleep*) So tired . . . all those little bells . . . uncle . . . dear mamma and uncle . . .

VARYA

Come, my darling, come.

Goes with ANYA *into Anya's room.*

TROFIMOV

(*emotionally*) My sunshine! My spring!

ACT TWO

Out in the fields. A chapel, old and tumbledown, long abandoned; an old bench. A road to Gaev's estate can be seen. To one side is a dark group of tall poplars: there the cherry orchard begins. In the distance is a row of telegraph poles. And far, far away, on the horizon, the vague outline of a large city, visible only in very good and clear weather. It is almost sunset. CHARLOTTA, YASHA, *and* DUNYASHA *are sitting on the bench.* YEPIHODOV *is near them, playing his guitar. Everyone is lost in his own thoughts.* CHARLOTTA *wears an old uniform cap. She has taken a rifle off her shoulders and adjusts the buckle on the strap.*

CHARLOTTA

(*dreamily*) I don't have a proper passport. I don't know how old I am. I think of myself as quite a young person. When I was a little girl, my father and mother used to travel from fairground to fairground, giving performances, and very good ones too. I used to do a trapeze act, amongst other things. When papa and mamma died a German lady took me into her home and started to give me lessons. Well, there you are! I grew up and became a governess. But where I come from and who I am—I don't know . . . Who my parents were—they weren't even married for all I know. (*Takes a cucumber out of her pocket and gnaws it*) . . . I don't know anything. (*Pause*) I long to have someone to talk to. But there's nobody. I haven't anyone.

YEPIHODOV

(*plays his guitar and sings*)

What is the whole world to you, love?
You care not for friends or for foes.
We will fly on the wings of our true love,
To the land where the passion fruit grows.

How nice it is to play the mandolin.

DUNYASHA

That's a guitar, not a mandolin. (*Looks in a pocket mirror and powders her face*)

YEPIHODOV

For a lunatic who is in love, this is a mandolin (*sighs*).

When I am alone with you, darling,
I'm timid, I'm speechless, it's true;
But surely in spite of my silence
You can feel all my passion for you.

YASHA *joins in the song.*

CHARLOTTA

Shocking! The way these people sing! Ugh! Howling jackals!

DUNYASHA

(*to* YASHA) All the same, how heavenly to have been abroad!

YASHA

Well, naturally. You're absolutely right. (*Yawns, lights cigar*)

YEPIHODOV

It's understandable. Abroad everything's been going in great style for ages.

YASHA

Well, naturally.

YEPIHODOV

I'm a thinking man. I've read a great many *extraordinary* books. But somehow I can't understand where things are going. What do I want? Am I to go on living or, to put it in a nutshell, shall I shoot myself? Just the same I always carry a gun. Look! (*Shows pistol*)

CHARLOTTA

(*referring to cucumber*) Finished! I'll go now. (*Slings rifle over her shoulder*) As for you, Yepihodov, you're a very clever man and a very frightening one; the women must be wild about you. Brr! (*Moving off*) These clever people are all so silly. There's no one for me to speak to . . . I'm all alone. Alone . . . There isn't anyone . . . And who I am, or why I am, nobody knows. (*Goes out slowly*)

YEPIHODOV

To speak absolutely precisely and come straight to the point, I am bound to say that among other things Fate treats me without mercy, as a storm tosses a little boat . . . Now, if, for the sake of argument, I am wrong, then why was it that this morning when I woke up, and just to give you an instance, there on my chest sits a spider of gigantic proportions. (*Shows with both hands*) Big as this. Another thing; I take a drink of kvass and what should there be at the bottom of the glass, if you please, but something indecent in the highest degree—such as a cockroach. (*Pause*) Have you read Buckle's *Natural History*? (*Pause, then to* DUNYASHA) May I please trouble you to let me have a word?

DUNYASHA

Go ahead.

YEPIHODOV

I would like to speak to you alone (*sighs*).

DUNYASHA

(*embarrassed*) Oh very well . . . but first of all would you bring my shawl. It's hanging behind the door . . . It's a bit chilly.

YEPIHODOV

Certainly. I'll get it. Now I know what to do with my gun. (*Takes his guitar, and goes out playing it*)

YASHA

"Never come singly"! Between you and me, he's a fool. (*Yawns*)

DUNYASHA

Please God he doesn't shoot himself. (*Pause*) I'm all on edge. I'm just a bundle of nerves. I've been with the gentry since I was a little girl and now I've got out of the old ways; look at my hands—white, ever so white, like a young lady's. I'm frightened of just everything . . . Everything's so terrifying. And Yasha, if you don't do the right thing by me, then I don't know what will happen to my nerves.

YASHA

(*kisses her*) Sugar! But let me tell you one thing! A person mustn't forget herself. If there's one thing I just hate it's a girl who misbehaves herself.

DUNYASHA

I'm madly in love with you—passionately. You're such an educated person. There's nothing you can't talk about. *Pause.*

YASHA

(*yawning*) Well, if you want to know what I think, if a girl lets herself fall in love with a person it means she's no better than she should be. (*Pause*) It's nice, smoking a cigar out of doors . . . (*Listening*) They're coming this way . . . (DUNYASHA *kisses him fervently*) Go home. Pretend you were having a swim in the river. Go this way—if they meet you what will they think about me? They'll think I'd arranged to meet you. I couldn't stand that.

DUNYASHA

(*coughing a little bit*) Your cigar is giving me a headache.

DUNYASHA *goes,* YASHA *stays, sits by the chapel;* RANEVSKAYA, GAEV, *and* LOPAHIN *come in.*

LOPAHIN

Listen: a decision must be made. Time waits for no man. It's as simple as this: will you or won't you let the land go for summer cottages? Answer in one word: yes or no—just one single word!

RANEVSKAYA

Someone's smoking—a horrid cheap cigar. (*Sits down*)

GAEV

Since they built the railroad, everything's so easy. (*Sits down*) We went into town and had our lunch . . . The yellow ball in the center! . . . I think I should like to go indoors and just have one game . . .

RANEVSKAYA

There's plenty of time.

LOPAHIN

Just a single word! (*Imploring*) Give me an answer!

GAEV

(*yawning*) What's that?

RANEVSKAYA

(*looking in her purse*) Yesterday there was quite a bit of money and today there's hardly any. My poor Varya scrimps and scrapes and gives us nothing but soup and in the servants' quarters the old people get nothing but dried peas. And here am I spending money like water . . . (*Drops the purse, gold pieces roll about; with irritation*) Oh look at that!

YASHA

Allow me. I'll pick them up in a second. (*Picks up the money*)

RANEVSKAYA

Oh do, Yasha. And why did I have to go out to lunch? That restaurant of yours was ghastly; the music! The tablecloths all smelling of soap . . . Need one drink so much, Leonid? Need one eat so much? Need one talk so much? Today in the restaurant you were talking away again—and quite unsuitably—about the seventies, about the Decadents—and to whom? I mean, imagine talking to waiters about the Decadents!

LOPAHIN

Yes!

GAEV

(*flapping his hands*) I'm incorrigible, that's quite clear . . . (*To* YASHA, *with irritation*) You're always underfoot!

YASHA

(*laughing*) I just can't help laughing at your voice.

GAEV

(*to his sister*) Look . . . either he goes or I.

RANEVSKAYA

Run along, Yasha; get away with you.

YASHA

(*returns her purse*) Right away. (*Trying not to laugh*) This very minute. (*Goes*)

LOPAHIN

Deriganov is planning to buy your estate. He's enormously rich. They say he'll come to the sale himself.

RANEVSKAYA

And where did you hear that?

LOPAHIN

They were talking about it in town.

GAEV

Our aunt from Yaroslav promised to send help. But when, and how much, who knows?

LOPAHIN

How much will she send? A hundred thousand? Two hundred?

RANEVSKAYA

Oh . . . We'd be very grateful for ten thousand or fifteen.

LOPAHIN

Excuse me, but in all my life I never met such feckless, unbusinesslike, extraordinary people as you! I tell you in words of one syllable that your estate is going to be sold and you don't seem to take it in.

RANEVSKAYA

But what are we to do? Tell us that?

LOPAHIN

I tell you every blessed day. I tell you the same thing over and over again. All the land, including the cherry orchard, must be let by the year for summer cottages. And this must be done now—as soon as possible. The sale is right on top of us! Do get this into your heads; once you've made up your minds that it should be summer cottages, you'll get all the money you want. You'll be saved.

RANEVSKAYA

Oh, summer cottages—and summer people—forgive me, it's so common.

GAEV

I agree with you entirely.

LOPAHIN

I shall either start to cry or I'll scream or I'll faint. This is the end! I can't take any more. (*To* GAEV) You're a silly old woman.

GAEV

What's that?

LOPAHIN

A silly old woman I said. (LOPAHIN *starts to go*)

RANEVSKAYA

No. No. Don't go away . . . Somehow with you here, it's more amusing . . . (*Pause*) I feel all the time as if something dreadful were going to happen . . . As if the house were going to tumble about our ears.

GAEV

(*deep in thoughts*) Double in the corner . . . Cannon off the cushion . . .

RANEVSKAYA

What sinners we've been!

LOPAHIN

What sort of sins have you committed?

GAEV

(*with candy in his mouth*) They say that I've gobbled up all my fortune in sweets! (*Laughs*)

RANEVSKAYA

Oh my sins . . . All my life I have spent money like wildfire, like a mad woman. I married a man who did nothing but get into debt. My husband dies—of champagne, he drank hideously—and then, for my undoing, I fell in love with another man. We came together, and at that very time—it was the first punishment—a blow right to the heart—in this very river . . . drowned . . . my little boy. I went abroad. I went away for good and all—never to return, never to see this river again . . . I shut my eyes and fled. Fled without a single thought. But he—followed me . . . a coarse man without mercy. I bought a villa on the Riviera because he had fallen ill there; and for three years neither day nor night did I know a single moment of peace. That sick man literally tore me apart. My soul shriveled up. A year ago I sold the villa to pay my debts and went to Paris; and there he absolutely fleeced me, and then went off with another woman. I tried to take poison . . . so stupid, so shameful . . . but then suddenly I felt myself drawn back to Russia, to my own country . . . to my girl. (*Wiping her eyes*) Oh God, God be merciful, forgive me my sins! Don't punish me any more. (*Takes a cable out of her pocket*) From Paris. I've done with Paris . . . He asks me to forgive him, implores me to come back. (*Tears up the cable*) Music, somewhere (*listening*).

GAEV

That's our celebrated Jewish Orchestra. Surely you remember—four violins, flute, and double bass.

RANEVSKAYA

Still going? They must come out here and play. We'll give a little evening.

LOPAHIN

(*listening*) I can't hear them. (*Hums softly, laughs*) Last night at the theatre I saw the funniest play.

RANEVSKAYA

I don't suppose it was the least bit funny. You shouldn't look at plays. You should just take a good look at yourself. Your life is dull! Such a lot of talk about unimportant things.

LOPAHIN

It's true. Better admit it frankly. Life here is stupid . . . (*Pause*) My old father was a peasant, a complete idiot. He didn't know anything about anything; he didn't teach me anything—all he did was to knock me about when he was drunk, and always with a stick. And as a matter of fact I'm just such another idiot and dunce. I never learnt anything, my handwriting is no better than a pig's: I am ashamed for people to see it.

RANEVSKAYA

You should get married, my friend . . .

LOPAHIN

Yes, that's true.

RANEVSKAYA

To our Varya. She's a good girl.

LOPAHIN

Yes.

RANEVSKAYA

She's a simple girl; works all day long. But the important thing is that she loves you and you've liked her for a long time.

LOPAHIN

Well, what about it? I'm not against it. She's a good girl.

Pause.

GAEV

I've been offered a position in a bank. The salary isn't bad . . . Had you heard?

RANEVSKAYA

You just stay right where you are.

FIRS *comes in with Gaev's overcoat.*

FIRS

(*to* GAEV) Please, sir—your overcoat. It's chilly.

GAEV

(*putting on coat*) I'm sick of you, my dear fellow.

FIRS

What next? . . . You left in the morning without a word. (*Looks him over*)

RANEVSKAYA

How old you've got, Firs!

FIRS

What's that?

LOPAHIN

They say you've got very old!

FIRS

I've been living a long time. They were trying to marry me off even before your father was born (*laughs*). By the time the serfs were set free I was head footman. I didn't take my freedom; I stayed with the family . . . (*Pause*) I remember how glad the people all were. But why? They didn't know why.

LOPAHIN

In the old days everything was just great. There were great floggings anyway.

FIRS

(*not hearing*) Yes, indeed. We belonged to them and they belonged to us. But now no one belongs to anyone. No one knows where they are.

GAEV

That'll do, Firs, thank you. I must go to town tomorrow. I was promised an introduction to a general who can arrange a loan for me.

LOPAHIN

Nothing will come of it . . . and, anyway, you wouldn't be able to pay the interest.

RANEVSKAYA

He's out of his mind. There are no generals.

TROFIMOV, ANYA, *and* VARYA *come in.*

GAEV

Here come the children.

ANYA

Here's mamma.

RANEVSKAYA

(*tenderly*) Well, darlings (*embraces* ANYA *and* VARYA). If only you two knew how I love you! Sit here beside me.

Everybody sits down.

LOPAHIN

Our perennial student always with the young ladies . . .

TROFIMOV

Not your business.

LOPAHIN

Almost fifty and still a student.

TROFIMOV

Don't try to be so funny.

LOPAHIN

Why are you so cranky?

TROFIMOV

Oh, leave me alone.

LOPAHIN

(*laughs*) Listen, let me ask you a question: what do you think of me?

TROFIMOV

Well, this is what I think of you: you're a rich man; you'll soon be a millionaire, and just as a ravenous wild beast, which devours all before it, is a necessary part of the natural process—so, my dear Yermolai Alexeyevich, are you.

All laugh.

VARYA

Petya, why don't you tell us something about the planets?

RANEVSKAYA

No; let's go on with what we were talking about yesterday.

TROFIMOV

What were we talking about?

GAEV

About human dignity.

TROFIMOV

We talked and talked yesterday, but we didn't get far. You said you thought that there was something mystical about human dignity. Well, maybe in your own way you are right. But if you look at it in a simple, straightforward way, what is the sense of human dignity? Suppose a person is a poor specimen of the human race, suppose, as happens more often than not, he is crude, stupid, deeply unhappy. He'd better not be too pleased with himself. What we have to do is work.

GAEV

All the same one has to die.

TROFIMOV

Who knows? And what does it mean—to die? It may very well be that a person has a hundred senses, and when he dies, only the five die which are known to us, and the other ninety-five are still alive.

RANEVSKAYA

What a clever boy you are, Petya!

LOPAHIN

(*ironically*) Oh incredibly!

TROFIMOV

Humanity is marching onward from strength to strength. What is unattainable now, one day we shall be able to achieve, able to understand. But now what we have to do is work; to give all the help we possibly can to those who seek the truth.

But now, here in Russia, only a handful of people are working. The vast majority of the intelligentsia—anyway of the ones I know—aren't seeking for anything, aren't doing anything. They aren't yet fit to work. Intelligentsia they call themselves. But they condescend to servants, treat the peasants like animals; they have no desire to learn; they don't read anything serious; they don't do a thing. They just chatter about science; and as to art—well, they hardly understand one thing about it. Oh, they're all intensely serious; they all go about with long faces; they only discuss the weightiest topics—philosophy and that. But, meantime, right under their noses, the working people are wretchedly fed, sleep on bare boards, thirty or forty to a room, which is verminous, stinking, damp, and morally squalid as well. So it looks as if all the grand talk is just a sop to our consciences.

Tell me this: what about all the care of children, which we're always hearing about? What about public libraries? Oh, they exist in novels all right; but not in reality. In reality all we have is degradation, barbarity, and filth. I'm afraid I have no patience with serious faces; they frighten me; and so does serious talk. Better be silent.

LOPAHIN

Do you know, I'm up and about at five o'clock in the morning each and every day. I work from dawn till dusk. And I always have money in my pocket—my own and other people's. It doesn't take you long to find out how few decent, honest people there are. Sometimes at night when I can't sleep, I think to myself: Dear God, I think, You have given us these immense forests, endless fields, limitless horizons and we who live in all this should be giants.

RANEVSKAYA

Oh, giants! They're all very fine in fairy tales. In real life they'd frighten one to death. (YEPIHODOV *passes in the background playing the guitar*) There goes Yepihodov (*absently*).

ANYA

(*absently*) There goes Yepihodov.

GAEV

Ladies and gentlemen, the sun has set.

TROFIMOV

Yes.

GAEV

(*gently declaiming*) Oh Nature, divine Nature, thou shinest with perpetual radiance, beautiful, indifferent. We call thee Mother. In thee are united Life and Death; by thee are we brought to life and by thee destroyed.

VARYA

(*pleading*) Uncle dear!

ANYA

Uncle dear!

TROFIMOV

You'd better cannon off the cushion.

GAEV

I'll hold my tongue. I'll hold my tongue.

Pause. Only the low mumbling of FIRS. *Suddenly from far off is heard an unearthly sound—the sound of a broken string, dying, sad.*

RANEVSKAYA

What's that?

LOPAHIN

I don't know. Somewhere, far off, a bucket has fallen in the mine. But far off.

GAEV

A bird of some sort? A heron?

TROFIMOV

Or an owl?

RANEVSKAYA

(*shuddering*) It's unpleasant; I don't know why.

Pause.

FIRS

It was just the same before the disaster; the owl hooted and the samovar hummed and no one knew why.

GAEV

Before what disaster?

FIRS

Before the serfs were set free.

Pause.

RANEVSKAYA

Let's go, friends. It's beginning to get dark. (*To* ANYA) There are tears in your eyes . . . what's the matter, darling? (*Embraces her*)

ANYA

It's nothing, mamma.

TROFIMOV

Somebody's coming.

A passer-by appears in an old, battered white military cap and overcoat. He is somewhat drunk.

PASSER-BY

Would you be good enough to tell me: is this the way to the railroad station?

GAEV

Yes it is. Through there.

PASSER-BY

Most grateful thanks (*coughs*). What glorious weather! (*Declaiming*) Oh my brother, my suffering brother . . . go to the Volga, whose constant murmur . . . (*To* VARYA) Mademoiselle, would you spare a little something for a hungry Russian?

VARYA *is frightened and cries out.*

LOPAHIN

(*angrily*) This is outrageous.

RANEVSKAYA

There! . . . Take this . . . (*looks in purse*) . . . no silver . . . never mind . . . take this.

PASSER-BY

My most grateful thanks. (*He goes*)

VARYA

I give up . . . I just give up. Mamma darling. There's nothing for the servants to eat and you gave him a gold piece!

RANEVSKAYA

What is to be done with me? I'm so silly. When we get back into the house I'll give you all I've got. Yermolai Alexeyevich, you'll make me another loan, won't you?

LOPAHIN

At your service.

RANEVSKAYA

Come on, children; time to go home. Varya, while you weren't looking, we made a match for you. Congratulations!

VARYA

(*through tears*) Don't make a joke of it, mamma.

LOPAHIN

Get thee to a nunnery, Amelia!

GAEV

My hands are itching. I haven't had a game for ages (*indicates billiards*).

LOPAHIN

Amelia, Nymph in thy something or other, be all my sins remembered.

RANEVSKAYA

Come on, children, let's go. Nearly time for supper.

VARYA

That man simply terrified me. My heart's still pounding.

LOPAHIN

Now don't forget . . . On August the twenty-second your cherry orchard goes up for sale. Think it over. Just think it over.

They all go, except TROFIMOV *and* ANYA.

ANYA

(*laughing*) We should be grateful to that man. He frightened Varya and now we're by ourselves.

TROFIMOV

Varya's afraid that we shall fall in love; so she never leaves us alone. Her narrow little mind can't comprehend that we're above love. To rise above petty unreal things which keep us from freedom and happiness—in that is the purpose of life, in that is its meaning. Onward! Undaunted, towards the brilliant star which shines far off! Onward! Let nothing hold you back, my friends.

ANYA

(*clapping her hands*) You just speak wonderfully! (*Pause*) It's so glorious today!

TROFIMOV

Yes, it's lovely weather.

ANYA

What have you done to me, Petya? Why don't I love the cherry orchard as I used? I loved it so much. I thought there was no better place on earth than our orchard.

TROFIMOV

All Russia is our orchard. The world is wide and wonderful and full of beautiful places. (*Pause*) Think, Anya: your grandfather, your great-grandfather, and all your ancestors—they were slave owners. They owned living souls. Can't you see that from every cherry in this orchard, from every leaf, from the trunk of every tree, human creatures are looking at you? Can't you hear their voices? . . . To own living souls . . . it has done something to all of you, those who lived before and those who are living now. So that your mother and you, and your uncle, no longer realize that your lives are being lived at the expense of others, of the very people whom you don't let inside the door . . . We are at least two hundred years behind the times. As yet we have nothing; no definite attitude to our past; we do nothing but philosophize; we grumble and are discontented, or else we just drink vodka. But it's perfectly clear. Before we can begin to live in the present we must atone for our past; we must make a break with it. But such atonement can only be achieved by suffering, only by tremendous, unremitting effort. You must understand this, Anya.

ANYA

The house we live in doesn't belong to us any more. It hasn't been ours for ages. I'll leave it. I promise I will.

TROFIMOV

Throw the keys into a deep well and go. Be free as the wind.

ANYA

(*exalted*) Oh, you said that so wonderfully!

TROFIMOV

Believe me, Anya, believe me! I'm not thirty yet. I'm young. I'm still a student, but I've been through a great deal. In the winter I am hungry, I am sick, I am anxious and as poor as a beggar. And wherever I go a cruel fate pursues me. Yet—always . . . at every minute, day or night, I feel a mysterious intimation. I feel an intimation of happiness, Anya. It's here . . .

ANYA

(*dreamily*) The moon is rising.

YEPIHODOV'S *guitar is heard—still the same song. The moon rises.* VARYA *is looking for* ANYA.

VARYA

(*offstage, calling*) Anya! Where are you?

TROFIMOV

Yes, the moon is rising. (*Pause*) Here it is. Happiness. It's coming. Nearer and nearer. I can hear it. And if we can't see it, if we don't recognize it, what does it matter? Others will see it.

VARYA

(*offstage*) Anya! Where are you?

TROFIMOV

Varya *again*! . . . (*Angrily*) It's outrageous!

ANYA

Oh well. Let's go down to the river. It's nice there.

TROFIMOV

Yes, let's go.

They go.

VARYA

(*offstage*) Anya! Anya!

ACT THREE

A drawing room and ballroom separated by an arch. A lighted chandelier. The Jewish Orchestra—previously mentioned in Act Two—is playing. A quadrille is in progress. Voice of SIMEONOFF-PISHCHIK: "Promenade à une paire!" *First couple to come into the drawing room is* SIMEONOFF-PISHCHIK *and* CHARLOTTA IVANOVNA, TROFIMOV *and* MADAME RANEVSKAYA *next, then* ANYA *and a post office employee, then* VARYA *with the station master.* VARYA *cries quietly, mopping her eyes as she dances.* DUNYASHA *is in the last couple.* PISHCHIK *shouts:* "Grand-rond, balancez" *and* "Les cavaliers à genoux et remerciez vos dames."

FIRS, *in a tailcoat, brings in soda water on a tray.* PISHCHIK *and* TROFIMOV *come into the drawing room.*

PISHCHIK

Ouf! Let me tell you one thing: I'm apoplectic. Yes; two strokes already. I shouldn't be dancing. But as the saying goes: if you're one of the pack you can bark or not bark but you *must* wag your tail. I'm as strong as a horse. My late progenitor used to make a joke of it—God rest his soul—he used to say that the ancient family of Simeonoff-Pishchik was descended from that very horse which Caligula made a Senator . . . (*sits down*) . . . but the dreadful thing is that there's no money! A hungry dog dreams of nothing but meat . . . (*snores, but wakes again at once*) . . . and that's how it is with me—only it's money.

TROFIMOV

You know, you do look a bit like a horse.

PISHCHIK

Oh well . . . a horse is a good animal. You can sell a horse . . .

The noise of billiards is heard from another room. VARYA *comes in.*

TROFIMOV

(*teasing*) Madame Lopahin! Madame Lopahin!

VARYA

(*vexed*) Seedy gent!

TROFIMOV

Yes, I am a seedy gent and proud of it.

VARYA

(*bitterly*) We've hired the musicians but how are we going to pay them? (*Goes out*)

TROFIMOV

If your entire life's energy hadn't been spent in scratching money together for the interest on your debts, you could have put it to some sensible purpose. Do you know what? You could have changed the face of the earth.

PISHCHIK

Nietzsche . . . the philosopher, don't you know . . . the

greatest, the most celebrated . . . a man of prodigious intellect . . . he says in one of his books . . . that it's all right apparently for a person to forge bank notes.

TROFIMOV

You've read Nietzsche?

PISHCHIK

Well—actually I got it from Dashenka. But now I'm in such a mess that there's no other way out but to forge bank notes . . . the day after tomorrow I have to pay three hundred and thirty rubles . . . I've saved up a hundred and . . . (*patting his pockets—in a panic*) the money's gone! . . . I've lost it! . . . (*Through tears*) Where's the money? (*Relieved*) Here it is! In the lining . . . do you know, I'm sweating.

RANEVSKAYA *and* CHARLOTTA *come in.*

RANEVSKAYA

(*humming gaily with the orchestra*) Why is Leonid so late? What is he doing in town? (*To* DUNYASHA) Dunyasha, do offer the musicians some tea.

TROFIMOV

I expect the sale has been called off.

RANEVSKAYA

What a moment to get the musicians here! What a moment to give a party! Oh well, it can't be helped. (*Sits down and hums quietly*)

CHARLOTTA

(*giving a deck of cards to* PISHCHIK) Here is a deck of cards. Think of a card.

PISHCHIK

I've thought of one.

CHARLOTTA

Now shuffle . . . Good. Give it to me, kind sir. *Ein, Zwei, Drei* . . . now look in your pocket . . .

PISHCHIK

(*takes card out of pocket*) Eight of spades. Absolutely right (*astonished*). Just fancy that!

CHARLOTTA

(*holding the deck on her palm, to* TROFIMOV) Quick! Which is the top card?

TROFIMOV

I don't know . . . Queen of spades?

CHARLOTTA

Queen of spades it is! (*To* PISHCHIK) You! which is the top card?

PISHCHIK

Ace of hearts.

CHARLOTTA

Ace of hearts it is! (*Claps her hands and the deck disappears*) What glorious weather we're having! (*A mysterious female voice replies as if from beneath the floor*) Yes, indeed, lovely lady, just glorious weather. (*In her own voice*) How captivating you are; you're my ideal! (*The voice*) And I'm enchanted by you, lovely lady!

STATION MASTER

(*applauding*) Bravo, the lady ventriloquist!

PISHCHIK

(*astonished*) Just fancy that! Charming! Charming! I'm in love with you.

CHARLOTTA

In love? (*Shrugging*) Can *you* fall in love? *Guter Mensch aber schlechter Musikant.*

TROFIMOV

(*patting* PISHCHIK *on the shoulder*) Dear old horse!

CHARLOTTA

Attention, please. One last trick. (*Takes a rug off a chair*) Now here's a thing, and a very pretty thing. I want to sell it . . . (*Shakes the rug*) Does anyone want to buy it?

PISHCHIK

(*astonished*) Oh just fancy that!

CHARLOTTA

Ein, Zwei, Drei! . . .

She whisks away the rug. ANYA *is behind it. She curtseys, runs to her mother, and embraces her; runs back amidst general enthusiasm.*

RANEVSKAYA

(*applauding*) Bravo! Bravo!

CHARLOTTA

Once again! *Ein, Zwei, Drei!* . . .

She whisks away the rug. VARYA *is behind it; she bows.*

PISHCHIK

(*astonished*) Oh, my goodness, just fancy that!

CHARLOTTA

That's all. (*Throws the rug over* PISHCHIK, *bows, and runs out*)

PISHCHIK

(*rushing after her*) Rogue! . . . Did you ever! . . . Rogue!

RANEVSKAYA

Still no sign of Leonid. Why is he so long in town? I can't understand it. It must be all over by now. The estate must be sold or else the sale never took place. Why must we be left in this suspense?

VARYA

(*trying to comfort her*) Darling uncle has bought it. I'm positive.

TROFIMOV

(*mocking*) Oh, of course.

VARYA

The great-aunt authorized him to buy the estate in her name—and to transfer the mortgage. She's doing it for Anya's sake. And I'm positive that, with God's help, darling uncle will buy it.

RANEVSKAYA

The great-aunt from Yaroslav has sent fifteen thousand to buy the estate in her name. She doesn't trust us. It's not even enough to pay the interest. (*Covers her face with her hands*) My fate will be decided today. Today.

TROFIMOV

(*teasing* VARYA) Madame Lopahin!

VARYA

(*angry*) Perennial student! You've been sacked from the University twice!

RANEVSKAYA

Why are you so cross, Varya? He's only teasing you about Lopahin. What of it? Marry him, if you want to. Why not? He's a good, interesting man. And if you don't want to, don't. Nobody's making you, darling.

VARYA

Mamma darling, this is serious to me. And one must be honest about it. He *is* a good man. I like him.

RANEVSKAYA

Then marry him. What are you waiting for? I don't understand.

VARYA

Mamma darling, I can't be the one to propose. For two years now everyone's been talking about him and me, everybody talks but he . . . doesn't say a word or else makes jokes. I can understand it. He's getting richer and richer, he's busy, he can't be bothered about me; if I had some money—not even a lot, just a little—I'd leave everything and go far away. I'd go to a convent.

TROFIMOV

That would be heaven!

VARYA

(*to* TROFIMOV) A student ought to be intelligent! (*Through tears*) How plain you've got, Petya, and so old! (*To* RANEVSKAYA) I've got to keep going, mamma darling. (*No longer crying*) I feel I've got to be doing something every moment of the day.

YASHA *comes in.*

YASHA

(*hardly able to contain his laughter*) Yepihodov has broken a billiard cue.

VARYA

Why is Yepihodov here? Who said he could play billiards? I simply cannot understand these people! (*She goes out*)

RANEVSKAYA

Don't tease her, Petya. Can't you see she's an unhappy girl?

TROFIMOV

She's a busybody. Poking her nose into other people's business; the whole summer long Anya and I have never had a moment's peace . . . Forever suspecting we were having a love affair. What business is that of hers? Besides there was nothing in it. I'm not interested in that kind of nonsense. We're above love.

RANEVSKAYA

And I suppose I'm beneath love. (*Agitated*) Why isn't Leonid here? If we only knew whether the estate had been sold, or no. The whole hideous business just seems beyond my comprehension. I don't know what to think. I'm just lost. At this moment, I could scream. I could do something idiotic. Save me, Petya, say something, anything.

TROFIMOV

What difference does it make whether the estate is sold today or not? It's all over. There's no turning back. It's the end of the road. Try not to worry. What's the good of deceiving yourself? For once in your life look the truth straight in the face.

RANEVSKAYA

But what is the truth? You can see what's true and what isn't. But I seem to be blind. I can't see anything. You take all sorts of important decisions so confidently. But tell me this, my dear: isn't that because you're young? Isn't it because you haven't had time to experience the agony which such decisions can cause? You look ahead so confidently. But isn't that because you can't see and you don't expect anything dreadful to happen? That's because you haven't come to grips with life—oh yes, you're more confident, more honest, more profound than we are. But look at it from my point of view and be as generous as ever you can. I was born here. My father and mother lived here; my grandfather. I love this house. I simply couldn't live without the cherry orchard. And if it has to be sold, you must sell me with it. (*She kisses* TROFIMOV *on the forehead*) My son was drowned here. (*Cries*) Have some pity for me, my dear man.

TROFIMOV

You know I feel for you with all my heart and soul.

RANEVSKAYA

But that's not the way to *say* it. (*Takes handkerchief out of her pocket; cable falls out*) Do you know, today I simply feel—crushed. You can have no idea. It's so noisy here—every sound jars on my nerves. I'm trembling. But I can't go away by myself. The silence frightens me. Don't think too badly of me, Petya . . . I love you as if you were one of my own family. I'd be perfectly willing to let you marry Anya—I promise. But, my dear boy, you must finish your studies, you must get your degree. You don't do a thing. Fate tosses you about from place to place. It's so odd . . . isn't it? Isn't it odd? And you must do something about that beard. Make it grow. (*Laughs*) You're so funny!

TROFIMOV

(*picking up cable*) I don't claim to be a beauty.

RANEVSKAYA

This is from Paris. I get one every day—yesterday—today. That wild creature is ill again. He implores me to forgive him and begs me to come to him; and I really ought to run over to Paris to be near him. You look so shocked, Petya. But my dear, what is one to do? What *shall* I do? He's ill, he's all alone, unhappy, who's to look after him? Who'll make him behave sensibly? Give him his medicine at the right times? Oh . . . what's the point of pretending; why not be open about it? I love him. It's quite obvious. I love him. I love him. He's a millstone around my neck; he's dragging me with him down to the depths. But I love my millstone. I can't live without him. (*Pressing* TROFIMOV's *hand*) Don't think badly of me, Petya. No, don't say anything. Please.

TROFIMOV

(*through tears*) Forgive me but I just must be honest. He fleeced you!

RANEVSKAYA

No. No. No. Don't say that . . . (*Puts her hands over her ears*)

TROFIMOV

He's just a rat, and you're the only person who doesn't know it. He's just a little insignificant, no-good rat.

RANEVSKAYA

(*angry, but controlled*) You're twenty-six years old—no, twenty-seven, but you sound like a schoolboy.

TROFIMOV

Very well. What of it?

RANEVSKAYA

It's time you grew up. At your age you ought to understand people who are in love. You ought to be in love yourself. You ought to fall in love. (*Angrily*) Yes, you ought. It's not purity in you, it's just priggishness. You're a prig. You're an ugly, ridiculous prig; do you know what you are? You're a freak.

TROFIMOV

(*horrified*) What is she saying?

RANEVSKAYA

"I'm above love." You're not above love. Our Firs has the right word for it. You're a silly young cuckoo. At your age you ought to have a mistress.

TROFIMOV

(*horrified*) This is frightful! What is she saying! (*Rushes to door of inner room, clutching his head*) It's frightful . . . I just can't . . . I'll faint. (*Dashes out but comes right back*) All is over between us! (*Dashes out of main door*)

RANEVSKAYA

(*shouting after him*) Petya! Wait! You silly, I was only joking! Petya!

(*In the hall are heard rushing feet on the stairs, then a crash.* ANYA *and* VARYA *cry out—then laugh.*) What is it? (ANYA *rushes in*)

ANYA

(*laughing*) Petya has fallen downstairs! (*Rushes out*)

RANEVSKAYA

What an old freak he is!

The station master comes to the middle of the inner room and starts to read "The Sinner" by Aleksei Konstantinovich Tolstoi. Everyone listens; but before he has read more than a few lines, a waltz starts up and the reading is broken off. Everyone dances. TROFIMOV, VARYA, ANYA, *and* RANEVSKAYA *come back into the room.*

RANEVSKAYA

Petya, darling, you're a dear, pure angel . . . Forgive me . . . let's dance. (*Dances with him*)

ANYA *and* VARYA *dance together.* FIRS *comes in, leaves his cane by the door.* YASHA *comes in too, watches the dancers.*

YASHA

What's the matter, grandpa?

FIRS

I don't feel well. In the old days, when we had a reception, generals, barons, admirals would be dancing here. But now we have to send for young fellows from the post office, station masters—and even they aren't extra pleased to come. I feel sort of feeble. The old master—these people's grandfather—used to dose everyone with sealing wax, whatever was wrong with them. I've been taking sealing wax every day for twenty years at least—much longer maybe; maybe that's why I'm still alive.

YASHA

I'm sick of you, gramps (*yawns*). I wish you'd drop dead.

FIRS

Ech you . . . silly young cuckoo . . . (*Mumbles*)

TROFIMOV *and* RANEVSKAYA *dance in.*

RANEVSKAYA

Merci! I'll rest. (*Sits down*) I'm tired.

ANYA *comes in.*

ANYA

(*agitated*) Out in the kitchen someone's been saying that the cherry orchard has been sold.

RANEVSKAYA

To whom?

ANYA

He didn't say. He went away again. (*Dances out with* TROFIMOV)

YASHA

It's just talk—some old man who came by—a stranger.

FIRS

Leonid Andreyevich still hasn't come back. And he's only got his light overcoat—his *demi-saison*. He'll catch a cold if he's not careful. Silly young fool!

RANEVSKAYA

I think I shall die. Yasha, go and find out who's bought it.

YASHA

The old man left hours ago. (*Laughs*)

RANEVSKAYA

(*irritated*) What is there to laugh at? What's funny about it?

YASHA

That Yepihodov! He's a scream! Gasbag! Old "Never come singly."

RANEVSKAYA

Firs, if the estate is sold, where will you go?

FIRS

I'll go wherever you tell me.

RANEVSKAYA

Are you all right? You don't look well. You ought to be in bed.

FIRS

Oh yes. In bed. And then who'll see to things? Who'll manage? There's nobody else in the whole house.

YASHA

Lyubov Andreyevna, may I please ask you something? Do me a favor. If you're going back to Paris, take me with you. Do please. It's just out of the question for me to stay here. (*Looking around to see that nobody overhears*) I *mean*! You can see for yourself, they're so ignorant here. They've no morals. And on top of it all, it's so boring. The food in the kitchen is simply uneatable. And, as if that weren't enough, this Firs—everywhere you go, always mumbling the stupidest things. Do take me with you. Please!

PISHCHIK *comes in.*

PISHCHIK

Permit me to ask you . . . a tiny waltz, my precious. (RANEVSKAYA *waltzes with him*) Nevertheless, charming lady, I must get a hundred and eighty rubles out of you . . . I shall, you know . . . a hundred and eighty . . . (*They dance into the inner room*)

YASHA

(*sings quietly*) "Could you but know my heart's unrest" . . .

In the inner room a figure in a top hat and check trousers appears capering about; shouts are heard of "Bravo, Charlotta Ivanovna, bravo!"

DUNYASHA

(*stopping to powder her face, speaking to* FIRS) My young ladies say I'm to dance. There are so many gentlemen and not enough ladies to go round, but I feel giddy when I dance and my heart pounds. Do you know, just now the young man from the post office said something that simply took my breath away.

Music gradually fades.

FIRS

What did he say to you?

DUNYASHA

"You're like a flower," he said.

YASHA

(*yawning*) Such ignorance! (*Goes*)

DUNYASHA

"Like a flower" . . . I'm such a sensitive little thing. I just love pretty speeches. I love them just terribly.

FIRS

Your head's turned.

YEPIHODOV *comes in.*

YEPIHODOV

(*to* DUNYASHA) So you don't want to see me. You look through me as if I were an insect of some kind. (*Sighs*) Such is life!

DUNYASHA

What do you want?

YEPIHODOV

No question; you're probably right (*sighs*). One thing is certain, if one looks at it from a point of view, so if you'll please excuse me for speaking very, very frankly, you've thrown me into a perfect state, actually. I know my luck, every day some kind of trouble happens to me. I've got used to it. It's been going on a long time. I can regard Destiny with a smile. You gave me your word, and although I . . .

DUNYASHA

Please. We'll talk about it later. Just now leave me alone. I want to daydream. (*Plays with her fan*)

YEPIHODOV

You know me. Troubles every day. Never come singly. And, if you'll allow me to say so, I just smile. I laugh even. (VARYA *comes in from inner room*)

VARYA

(*to* YEPIHODOV) Still here? Such cheek! (*To* DUNYASHA) Run along, Dunyasha. (*To* YEPIHODOV) First of all you play billiards and break a cue, then you hang about the drawing room like one of the guests . . .

YEPIHODOV

Don't you carp at me. If I may say so, you can't do such a thing.

VARYA

I'm not carping at you, I'm just telling you. You do nothing but stroll around the place—not a stroke of work. I simply don't know why we keep you as a clerk.

YEPIHODOV

(*offended*) Whether I work, or whether I stroll around, or whether I eat or play billiards is for people to discuss who have some sense and who are older . . .

VARYA

How dare you! How dare you speak like that to me! (*Flaring up*) Do you mean that I have no sense? Get out of here! This very minute.

YEPIHODOV

I must ask you not to take that tone.

VARYA

(*beside herself*) This very minute. Out you go! Out! (*He goes toward the door; she follows him*) "Never come singly." Don't let me catch you coming back. I don't want to set eyes on you ever again! (YEPIHODOV *goes; his voice is heard offstage:* "I shall lodge a complaint about this") Coming back are you? (*Seizes Firs's cane which is at the door*) Very well. Come on then. Come on. I'll show you . . . Are you coming or aren't you? Well? All right. Take that! (*She lifts the cane and* LOPAHIN *comes in*)

LOPAHIN

My most respectful thanks.

VARYA

(*crossly and ironically*) Very sorry, I'm sure.

LOPAHIN

It's nothing. My most respectful thanks for a delightful welcome.

VARYA

Don't mention it. (*Moving away, then looking back and asking gently*) I didn't hurt you, did I?

LOPAHIN

It's nothing. There's a huge bruise coming up, that's all.

Voices in the inner room: "Lopahin has come," "Yermolai Alexeyevich is here."

PISHCHIK

Here's himself as large as life and twice as natural. (*Hugs* LOPAHIN; *then sniffs*) Hm! Cognac! We're having a high old time here too.

RANEVSKAYA *comes in.*

RANEVSKAYA

You, Yermolai Alexeyevich! What's kept you? Where is Leonid?

LOPAHIN

(*embarrassed; trying not to show his excitement*) The sale was over by four o'clock. We missed the train. We had to wait till the nine thirty. (*Deep sigh*) Ough! (*Hand to forehead*) I feel a bit dizzy.

GAEV *comes in, packages in his right hand; he wipes his eyes with the other hand.*

RANEVSKAYA

Well, Leonid? What . . . ? For God's sake tell us.

GAEV *does not answer; just gestures with his hand.*

GAEV

(*to* FIRS, *through tears*) Here take these . . . anchovies, and Kertsch herrings. I haven't had a bite to eat all day . . . What I've been through! (*From the billiard room the click of the balls is heard.* YASHA'*s voice:* "Seven and eighteen!" GAEV'*s expression changes; he stops crying.*) I'm tired out.

Firs, come and help me change. (*Goes out followed by* FIRS)

PISHCHIK

What happened at the sale? Tell us.

RANEVSKAYA

Is the orchard sold?

LOPAHIN

Sold.

RANEVSKAYA

Who bought it?

LOPAHIN

I did. (*Pause.* RANEVSKAYA *is overwhelmed.* VARYA *takes the keys from her belt, throws them into the middle of the room, and goes out.*) I bought it! Wait a minute. I'm dizzy. I can't speak . . . (*Laughs*) When we got to the sale, Deriganov was there already. Leonid Andreyevich had no more than fifteen thousand, but Deriganov bid thirty thousand straight away, over and above the mortgage. I saw how things were and jumped right in—forty thousand. Forty-five, bids Deriganov. Fifty-five, I said. He goes to sixty. Seventy, I said. Every time he went up by five I jumped him ten. Suddenly it was all over. In the end it was knocked down to me at ninety thousand. The cherry orchard is mine now! Mine! (*Laughing uproariously*) My God! . . . Dear God Almighty, the cherry orchard is mine! Tell me I'm drunk, tell me I'm raving mad, tell me it isn't really happening. (*Stamps his feet*) Don't laugh at me! If only my father, my grandfather, could rise from the dead and could see all this, how their Yermolai, the little boy they used to thrash, who could hardly read or write, how their Yermolai, who went barefoot in winter, how this same

Yermolai has bought the finest estate in the whole world. I've bought the estate where my father and grandfather were serfs; where they weren't even allowed into the kitchen. I'm asleep . . . it hasn't really happened . . . You're just imagining it. It's just part of the mysterious half-light in which we live. (*Picks up the keys, smiling kindly*) She threw down the keys. She wanted to show that she's no longer the mistress . . . (*Jingles keys*) Well, what of it? (*Orchestra tunes up*) Hey, musicians, play up. Let me hear you! You must come, all of you, and see how Yermolai Alexeyevich will take the axe to the cherry orchard. The trees will come crashing down! Up will go summer cottages; and our grandchildren and their grandchildren will see a new life . . . Music! Play up! (*Music.* RANEVSKAYA *has collapsed on a chair and is crying.*) Why, oh why didn't you listen to me? Too late now, my poor dear. (*Through tears*) If only it could all be over soon. If only our muddled, unhappy lives could somehow be changed.

PISHCHIK

(*taking him by the arm; in a low tone*) She's crying. Let's go into the other room. She'd rather be alone . . . Come. (*They move off*)

LOPAHIN

What's the matter? Music! Louder! Everything must be as I wish it. (*Ironically*) Here comes the new master, here comes the owner of the cherry orchard! (*Accidentally he upsets a table, almost throwing down the candelabra*) I can pay for everything . . . (*He and* PISHCHIK *go out*)

Nobody is left except RANEVSKAYA *sitting in a crumpled heap, crying bitterly. The orchestra is heard offstage.* ANYA *goes to her mother and kneels.* TROFIMOV *stays near the door of the other room.*

ANYA

Mamma . . . mamma, don't cry . . . My dear darling, sweet, kind mamma, I love you. God bless you, darling. The cherry orchard is sold; it's over; that's true, that's true. But don't cry, mamma. You still have your life ahead of you . . . You're still your dear, wonderful self . . . come with me, come dearest; we'll go away! We'll plant a new orchard, a lovelier one; you'll live to see it; you'll know what it means. And happiness, deep, peaceful happiness will be all around you like evening sunshine. You'll be able to smile again, my own dear mamma! Come along my darling! Come . . .

ACT FOUR

Same as Act One, but no curtains on the windows, no pictures. A few pieces of furniture are left which have been pushed into corners as if ready for sale. An emptiness is felt. Near the outer door, luggage, bundles, and so on. The inner door to the left is open and from there voices of VARYA *and* ANYA *can be heard.* LOPAHIN *is standing about.* YASHA *holds a tray with filled champagne glasses. In the entrance hall* YEPIHODOV *ties a trunk. In the background are heard voices of peasants, servants who have come to bid good-bye.* GAEV*'s voice is heard:* "Thank you, friends, thank you."

YASHA

The people about the place have come to say good-bye. Do you know what I think, Yermolai Alexeyevich? Our people are good but they haven't any sense.

Voices are heard; they die away; RANEVSKAYA *and* GAEV *come in from outside. She is composed but pale, her face trembles, she can hardly speak.*

GAEV

You gave them your purse. You shouldn't have done that, you really shouldn't.

RANEVSKAYA

I couldn't help it. I just had to. (*They go*)

LOPAHIN

(*to their retreating figures*) Please. Just one glass—just to say farewell. I didn't think of bringing it out from town and I could only get one bottle at the station. Please! (*Pause*) No? (*Returns from door*) If I'd known you wouldn't accept it, I wouldn't have bought it. Oh well, I won't have any either. (YASHA *carefully places the tray on a chair*) You have one, Yasha, anyway.

YASHA

Here's to those who are leaving and to those who are staying behind! (*Drinks*) This isn't proper champagne, I can tell you that.

LOPAHIN

Eight rubles a bottle. (*Pause*) It's as cold as the devil.

YASHA

The stoves weren't lit today. After all, we're going away. (*Laughs*)

LOPAHIN

What's the joke?

YASHA

I'm laughing for joy.

LOPAHIN

It's October already; but it's still and golden like summer. Just the weather for building. (*Looks at watch and speaks toward the door*) Please remember the train will leave in forty-six minutes! We must leave for the station in twenty minutes. So hurry up!

TROFIMOV *enters from main door in overcoat.*

TROFIMOV

Isn't it time we were going? The carriage is ready. The devil alone knows where my galoshes are. They've disappeared. (*Shouts through inner door*) Anya, my galoshes aren't here! I can't find them anywhere!

LOPAHIN

I've got to go to Kharkov. I'll go in your train. I'll spend all winter in Kharkov. I've just been hanging around here all this time. I'm sick of having no work to do. I can't bear not to be working. I don't even know what to do with my hands; they just flap at my sides, as if they were somebody else's hands.

TROFIMOV

Let's be off now. And you can get busy with useful work again.

LOPAHIN

Have some.

TROFIMOV

Not for me (*indicating champagne*).

LOPAHIN

You're off to Moscow, I suppose.

TROFIMOV

Yes, I'll go with them to town and on to Moscow tomorrow.

LOPAHIN

Yes; I imagine the professors will hardly begin their lectures until you get there.

TROFIMOV

Not your business.

LOPAHIN

How many years have you been up at the University?

TROFIMOV

Think of something new for a change. That's old and cheap. (*Looks for galoshes*) You know very likely you and I won't see each other again. So let me give you a last piece of advice: don't keep flapping your hands about. Get out of the habit of flapping. And another thing: building summer cottages on the assumption that the summer visitors will eventually buy their houses and cultivate their land—well, that's just flapping too . . . But never mind; in spite of everything I'm really quite fond of you. You have the hands of an artist. And I believe you have the soul of an artist.

LOPAHIN

(*hugs him*) Good-bye, my dear man, thank you for everything. Look, you may need a little money on the journey . . .

TROFIMOV

What for? I don't need it.

LOPAHIN

But you don't have any.

TROFIMOV

Oh yes I do. Thank you. I've just been paid for a translation. It's here. (*Indicates money in pocket; worried*) But I can't find my galoshes.

VARYA

(*offstage*) Here! Take the filthy things! (*Throws them into the room*)

TROFIMOV

Why are you so cross, Varya? Oh! These aren't mine!

LOPAHIN

Last spring I sowed a thousand acres of poppies, and now I've cleared forty thousand net. And when my poppies were in flower—what a picture that was! But what I mean was I cleared forty thousand so you see I can make you a loan. Why do you turn your nose up at it? I'm a plain peasant and I'm making a plain offer.

TROFIMOV

Your father was a peasant, mine was a pharmacist—what difference does it make? (LOPAHIN *takes out his wallet*) Put it away, I wouldn't take it if you gave me two hundred thousand. I'd rather stand on my own feet. All the grandeur and importance which you people value so much, whether you're rich or not, all that doesn't mean anything more to me than—a feather blown about by the wind. I can do without you. I can afford to ignore you. I'm strong and proud. Humanity is marching towards the most exalted truth, the most exalted happiness possible on earth; and I'm in the front rank.

LOPAHIN

Will you get there?

TROFIMOV

Yes. I will. (*Pause*) I'll get there and I'll show other people how to get there too.

Far away is heard the sound of axes cutting the trees.

LOPAHIN

Well, good-bye, my dear man. It's time. You and I look at each other down our noses: meantime life's passing by. When I'm really hard at work, I don't have time to feel tired or depressed. And then I seem to know the purpose of *my* existence too. How many people there are in Russia

—don't you agree, my dear fellow?—and none of them has the least notion of why he exists. Oh well, what of it? They say that Leonid Andreyevich has taken that post at the bank. The salary's quite good . . . but he won't keep it. He's too lazy.

ANYA

(*at the door*) Mamma says will you please not cut the trees down till after she's gone.

TROFIMOV

Yes, a little tact would have done no harm. (*Goes out through the main door*)

LOPAHIN

Of course, of course . . . what fools! (*Follows* TROFIMOV)

ANYA

Has Firs been taken to the hospital?

YASHA

I spoke about it this morning. I suppose he has.

ANYA

(*to* YEPIHODOV, *who crosses the stage*) Will you please find out if Firs has been taken to the hospital.

YASHA

(*offended*) I told Yepihodov to see to it this morning. Why do you have to ask ten times?

YEPIHODOV

Firs is such an old man that, if you want my last word on the subject, it's hopeless to try to patch him up. He'd better go the way of his forefathers. And, for my part, I can only envy him. (*Puts a heavy case on a hatbox and crushes it*) There you are! (*Goes out*)

YASHA

(*in a superior tone*) "Never come singly."

VARYA

(*offstage*) Has Firs been taken to the hospital?

ANYA

(*with a letter in her hand*) Yes, he has.

VARYA

But why didn't they take the letter to the doctor?

ANYA

We'll have to send it after him. (ANYA *goes out*)

VARYA

(*offstage*) Where is Yasha? Tell him his mother has come to say good-bye to him.

YASHA

(*with a gesture*) They make me tired.

During the foregoing DUNYASHA *has been busy with the luggage. Now that* YASHA *is alone she comes to him.*

DUNYASHA

If you'd only look at me, Yasha, just once. You are going away . . . You're leaving me. (*Cries and throws her arms round his neck*)

YASHA

What's the use of crying? (*Drinks champagne*) In six days I'll be in Paris again. Tomorrow we shall be in the Express. We'll be gone for good. It's almost too good to be true. I can hardly believe it. *Vive la France!* . . . This place is not for me. I can't live here. Oh well, it can't be helped. (*Drinks champagne*) What's the use of crying? Behave yourself, you won't cry then.

DUNYASHA

(*looking in the hand mirror and powdering herself*) Write to me from Paris. I loved you so much, Yasha, so much! I'm a sensitive little person, Yasha!

YASHA

They're coming.

Busies himself with luggage; hums. RANEVSKAYA, GAEV, ANYA, *and* CHARLOTTA *come in.*

GAEV

We should be going. Not much time left. (*Looking at* YASHA) Who's smelling of herring?

RANEVSKAYA

In ten minutes we must be in the carriage . . . (*Looks around the room*) Good-bye, my dear old house. Winter will end, spring will come, and you won't be there; you will have been torn down. How many things these walls have seen! (*Kisses* ANYA *fervently*) My precious, you look radiant; your eyes are sparkling like diamonds. Are you happy? Are you so very happy?

ANYA

Very. A new life is beginning, mamma.

GAEV

(*gaily*) Yes; everything's for the best. Before the cherry orchard was sold, we were all anxious, miserable, but then when matters were settled, irrevocably, once and for all, everybody accepted the situation and became quite cheerful again . . . I'm an employee in a bank, I'm a financier . . . yellow in the center . . . and as for you, sister, don't know why, but there's no question that you're looking better.

RANEVSKAYA

Yes. My nerves are better—I feel calmer, it's true. (*Her overcoat and hat are passed to her*) I'm sleeping well. Take my things out, Yasha, it's time. (*To* ANYA) We shall see one another soon, my dear child, but now I must go to Paris.

We shall live there on the money which your great-aunt at Yaroslav sent to buy the estate—praise be to the great-aunt! But of course it won't last long.

ANYA

Mamma, you'll come back soon, won't you? I'll work hard and pass my exams and then I'll get something to do and be able to help you. Mamma, we'll read all sorts of books together, you and I, won't we . . . (*Kisses her mother's hands*) We'll read in the long autumn evenings, read and read, and a new wonderful world will open up to us. (*In a dreamy tone*) You will come back, mamma.

RANEVSKAYA

Yes, my treasure, I will. (*Hugs her*)

LOPAHIN *comes in with* CHARLOTTA, *who is humming a song.*

GAEV

Listen to Charlotta! She's happy.

CHARLOTTA

(*rolls up a rug to look like a baby*) Baby's gone s'eepy byes! (*A baby is heard to cry* "Wah! Wah!") I'm so sorry for you. You break my heart. (*Throws the rug aside and in her own voice*) Please, you simply must find me a situation, you simply must.

LOPAHIN

We will, Charlotta Ivanovna, don't worry.

GAEV

Everyone is leaving us. Varya's going away . . . Nobody needs us any more.

CHARLOTTA

I don't know where I'm to stay in town. It's time we were off . . . (*hums*) Oh well!

PISHCHIK *comes in.*

LOPAHIN

Behold, the Wonder of the World!

PISHCHIK

(*out of breath*) Oh, just let me catch my breath . . . I'm utterly finished . . . my dear friends . . . water, please.

GAEV

He's after money, we may be quite sure. Your obedient servant will slip away from danger. (*He goes*)

PISHCHIK

Haven't been here for quite a time, gracious lady . . . (*To* LOPAHIN) You here? Take this! (*Gives money to* LOPAHIN) Four hundred; and another eight hundred and forty to come.

LOPAHIN

(*shrugging in astonishment*) It's like a dream . . . where did you get it?

PISHCHIK

Wait! It's not . . . an extraordinary occurrence. Some Englishmen came and found some kind of white clay on my land. (*To* RANEVSKAYA) For you too, four hundred . . . delightful, gracious lady . . . (*Gives money*) More, later. (*Drinks water*) Just now a young man on the train said that some . . . great philosopher advises jumping off the roof . . . "Jump" he said. That's the way to solve every problem. (*Astonished*) Just fancy that! Water, please.

LOPAHIN

What kind of Englishmen?

PISHCHIK

I rented them the piece of land with the clay for twenty-four years. But now, excuse me, I'm in a hurry, I must gallop . . . I've got further to go . . . I must go to Znoykov

. . . to Kardamanov . . . I owe money all round. (*Drinks water*) God bless you all . . . I'll drop in on Thursday.

RANEVSKAYA

But we're just off to town; and tomorrow I go abroad.

PISHCHIK

What? (*Greatly agitated*) Why to town? Oh yes . . . just look at the furniture . . . luggage . . . well, it can't be helped (*through tears*) . . . can't be helped . . . gigantic intelligence, those people, those Englishmen . . . it can't be helped . . . all the very best to you . . . God will help you . . . it can't be helped . . . in this world everything has to come to an end. (*Kisses* RANEVSKAYA'S *hand*) If ever word should reach you that my end has come, remember this . . . horse, and say: once there lived a man called Simeonoff-Pishchik, the Kingdom of Heaven be his . . . what wonderful weather . . . yes. (*He goes in great embarrassment, but comes back at once and says at the door*) My Dashenka sends her love. (*He goes*)

RANEVSKAYA

We can go now. But there are two things: first, Firs being so ill. (*Looks at watch*) We still have five minutes.

ANYA

Mamma, Firs has been taken to the hospital. Yasha saw to it.

RANEVSKAYA

The second thing is—Varya. She's used to being up early, to working all day long, and now with no work she's like a fish out of water. She's lost weight; she's pale; and cries, poor thing, all the time. (*Pause*) You know perfectly well, Yermolai Alexeyevich, I always dreamed of . . . giving her to you, and it always looked as if you and she were going to get married. (*Whispers to* ANYA, *who makes a sign to* CHARLOTTA *and both go out*) She loves you, you like her, and I don't know, I simply do not know why you seem to avoid each other. I can't understand it.

LOPAHIN

I can't understand it myself, to be perfectly frank. It's all so strange . . . if there's still time, I'm quite ready . . . Let's get it over and done with. I don't feel that, after you've gone, I shall be able to ask her.

RANEVSKAYA

Splendid. It won't take more than a moment. I'll call her now.

LOPAHIN

And we've got the champagne here—so appropriate. (*Looks at the glasses*) Empty . . . somebody's drunk it all up. (YASHA *coughs*) Swilled it all down, rather.

RANEVSKAYA

(*gaily*) Splendid! We'll go out . . . Yasha, *allez*! I'll call her. (*In doorway*) Varya, drop everything. Come here. Come! (RANEVSKAYA *and* YASHA *go out*)

LOPAHIN

(*looking at watch*) Yes . . .

Pause. Offstage one hears giggles, whispering, finally VARYA *is pushed in.*

VARYA

(*searching about*) Funny, I can't find it.

LOPAHIN

What are you looking for? (*Pause*) Where are you off to now?

VARYA

I? To the Ragulins . . . We've arranged that I shall look after things there—a sort of housekeeper, in a way.

LOPAHIN

The Ragulins? That's at least seventy miles away. (*Pause*) Well, life in this house is over.

VARYA

(*searching about again*) Where can it be? Perhaps I put it in a trunk . . . Yes, life in this house has come to an end . . . there'll be no more life here.

LOPAHIN

I'm just off to Kharkov on this train. I've a lot of business. I'm leaving Yepihodov to look after things. I've hired him.

VARYA

Oh yes?

LOPAHIN

This time last year we had snow by this time. Remember? And now it's still and golden . . . cold though . . . at least three degrees of frost.

VARYA

I didn't look. Besides our thermometer's broken . . .

Pause. A voice from out of doors is heard: "Yermolai Alexeyevich!"

LOPAHIN

(*as if he had been expecting this call all the time*) Coming! (*Goes out quickly*)

VARYA *sits on the floor, puts her head on a bundle, and cries quietly. The door opens.* RANEVSKAYA *tiptoes in.*

RANEVSKAYA

Well? (*Pause*) Time we were leaving.

VARYA

(*not crying any more*) Yes, it's time, mamma darling. I'll still get to the Ragulins today, if we don't miss the train.

RANEVSKAYA

(*calling toward doorway*) Anya, get your coat on!

ANYA *comes in, then* GAEV *and* CHARLOTTA, GAEV *in a heavy traveling coat. Servants come in.* YEPIHODOV *fusses around the luggage.*

RANEVSKAYA

Now we can be on our way.

ANYA

(*joyously*) On our way!

GAEV

My friends, my dear, kind friends! Can I leave this house forever and keep silent? Can I restrain myself? I must on this occasion give expression to the feelings which are welling up from the depth of my being . . .

ANYA

(*pleadingly*) Uncle!

VARYA

Uncle dear, don't.

GAEV

(*sadly*) Yellow to the center . . . I'll hold my tongue.

TROFIMOV *comes in; then* LOPAHIN.

TROFIMOV

Well, time we were leaving!

LOPAHIN

Yepihodov, my coat!

RANEVSKAYA

I'll sit a moment longer. It's as if I'd never noticed before what the walls are like and the ceiling. And now I look at them so hungrily, with such deep love.

GAEV

I remember when I was six years old, it was on Trinity Sunday; I sat in this window and watched father starting for church.

RANEVSKAYA

Has everything been taken out?

LOPAHIN

Looks like it. (*To* YEPIHODOV *as he puts on his coat*) See that everything is in order, Yepihodov.

YEPIHODOV

(*hoarse voice*) Certainly, certainly, Yermolai Alexeyevich.

LOPAHIN

What's happened to your voice?

YEPIHODOV

I just had a drink of water and something went down the wrong way.

YASHA

Such ignorance!

RANEVSKAYA

We shall go and there won't be a soul left behind.

LOPAHIN

Till the spring.

VARYA

(*takes a parasol from a bundle and it looks as if she were going to hit* LOPAHIN *with it;* LOPAHIN *pretends to be afraid*) I'm not going to hurt you . . . I didn't even think of it.

TROFIMOV

Come on! It's time! The train will be in any minute.

VARYA

Petya! Here they are! Your galoshes! (*In tears*) How old they are—and filthy!

TROFIMOV

(*putting on the galoshes*) Let's go, people.

GAEV

(*confused; trying not to weep*) Train . . . railroad station . . . cannon off the cushion . . . red on the spot.

RANEVSKAYA

Let's go.

LOPAHIN

Everybody here? Nobody left behind? (*Closes door to inner part of house*) Everything is stored in there. Better be locked up. Let's go!

ANYA

Good-bye, house! Good-bye, old life!

TROFIMOV

(*goes out with* ANYA) Welcome, new life!

VARYA *looks around the room; goes out without haste.* YASHA *and* CHARLOTTA, *with her dog, go out.*

LOPAHIN

Well, till the spring. (*To* RANEVSKAYA *and* GAEV) Don't be long . . . Bye-bye. (*Goes out*)

RANEVSKAYA *and* GAEV *are left alone. It is as if they had waited for this moment. They cling together and weep quietly as if afraid to be overheard.*

GAEV

(*in despair*) My sister! My sister!

RANEVSKAYA

My wonderful, wonderful, wonderful orchard. My life, my youth, my happiness—good-bye! . . . Good-bye!

ANYA's *voice calling gaily:* "Mamma." TROFIMOV's *voice, gay and excited:* "A-OO!"

RANEVSKAYA

One last look at the walls, the windows . . . dear mother used to love this room . . .

GAEV

My sister . . . my sister . . .

ANYA's *voice:* "Mamma." TROFIMOV's *voice:* "A-OO!"

RANEVSKAYA

(*calling*) Coming! (*They go*)

The stage is empty. The sound is heard of doors being slammed, then locked, then of the carriages leaving. Silence. In the silence, the dull thud of an axe upon a tree. Footsteps are heard. FIRS *appears from the inner door. As always, he is in his jacket and white vest but he is in slippers. He is ill.*

FIRS

(*goes to main door and rattles the handle*) Locked. They've gone . . . (*Sits on sofa*) They forgot me . . . oh well . . . I'll just rest here. One thing; Leonid Andreyevich didn't take his fur coat. Bet you he's gone off in his light coat . . . (*Sighs, in a worried manner*) I should have seen to it. Silly young . . . (*Mumbles unintelligibly*) Life has passed by as if I hadn't lived . . . (*Lies down*) I'll lie down . . . You've no strength left—you've nothing left—nothing . . . ech! You're a silly young cuckoo.

A sound is heard far off, as if the string of a violin were broken. A sad sound and a dying one. Silence. No sound except far away in the orchard the axes against the trees.

From Chekhov's Letters

EXCERPTS FROM CHEKHOV'S LETTERS

TRANSLATED BY LEONID KIPNIS

March 7, 1901

TO OLGA KNIPPER:

My next play will most certainly be funny, very funny, at least in conception.

April 22, 1901

TO OLGA KNIPPER:

An enormous desire comes sometimes upon me to write for the Moscow Art Theatre a vaudeville or a comedy in four acts. And I will write it if nothing comes in between. But I will give it to the theatre not before the end of 1903.

September 19, 1901

TO OLGA KNIPPER:

I will write a play for Artem. By all means he must be on the river fishing; and Vishnevsky must swim—splash—and speak loudly.*

* Artem played Firs in the first production of *The Cherry Orchard.* Chekhov intended the part of Gaev for Vishnevsky.

EXCERPTS FROM CHEKHOV'S LETTERS

December 18, 1901

TO OLGA KNIPPER:

I still dream of writing a funny play . . . where the devil will be a dragonfly. I don't know if anything will come of it.

January 20, 1902

TO OLGA KNIPPER:

I didn't write to you about the future play not because I have no faith in you, as you write, but because there is not yet faith in the play. It just begins to dawn little by little in my brain—as a very early dawn. I myself cannot understand what will become of it and it changes every day. Could we have met in person I would have told you all about it, but I cannot write because there is nothing to write about, only chatter, nonsense, and then I will cool on the subject.

March 16, 1902

TO OLGA KNIPPER:

I don't write my play and have no desire to, since there are many drama scribes now and it becomes tedious and common.

April 27, 1902

TO OLGA KNIPPER:

I will not write a play—my heart is not in it; and if I write something resembling a play, it will be a vaudeville in one act.

October 1, 1902

TO KONSTANTIN STANISLAVSKY:

I will be in Moscow on October 15 and will then explain to you why my play is not yet ready. I have a subject, but as yet not enough gunpowder, which is missing.

EXCERPTS FROM CHEKHOV'S LETTERS

October 8, 1902

TO OLGA KNIPPER:

You are out of your mind! ! ! To write a vaudeville for Moscow Art Theatre! Vaudeville with one character who only speaks but doesn't act at all! ! I'll write a play for the Theatre; it will be much better!

December 22, 1902

TO OLGA KNIPPER:

I want terribly to write a vaudeville, but there is never time. I just am not able to sit down. I have some kind of feeling that vaudeville will soon be popular again.

December 24, 1902

TO OLGA KNIPPER:

My "Cherry Orchard" will be in three acts. So it seems to me, but for the rest I have not made a final decision. As soon as I am well again I will make decisions; now I cast everything beyond.

January 1, 1903

TO KONSTANTIN STANISLAVSKY:

I will begin to write the play in February, at least I think so. I will come to Moscow with the finished play.

January 3, 1903

TO OLGA KNIPPER:

I wanted "Cherry Orchard" to be in three long acts, but I can make it four, it is all the same to me. Three or four acts —it still will be the same play.

EXCERPTS FROM CHEKHOV'S LETTERS

January 23, 1903

TO OLGA KNIPPER:

I received today a letter from Nemirovich-Danchenko. He asks about the play. That I will write a play is as certain as twice two is four, but certainly only if I get well. Will it succeed, will it amount to anything—I don't know.

January 27, 1903

TO KOMISSARJEVSKAYA*:

1. The play is conceived, it's true, and I even have a title ("Cherry Orchard"—but for the time being it is a secret) and I'll begin to write probably not later than the end of February if I am well. 2. The central part in the play is an old woman—to the author's chagrin.

February 5, 1903

TO KONSTANTIN STANISLAVSKY:

I count on beginning the play after February 20—and will finish it by March 20. The play is ready in my mind. It is called "The Cherry Orchard." Four acts; in the first there are cherry trees in blossom visible through the window; the whole garden white—and ladies in white gowns.

February 11, 1903

TO OLGA KNIPPER:

I will begin to write the play on February 21. You will play the foolish one. But then who will play the old mother? Who?

* Komissarjevskaya was a leading actress in St. Petersburg, who was trying to get the play for her theatre.

EXCERPTS FROM CHEKHOV'S LETTERS

February 11, 1903

TO LILINA*:

I was ill but now I am recovered, although today I am coughing again and have been lazy. I haven't yet begun the play, will do so after February 20, but in absolute hope that YOU will be in my play. I don't know how the play will turn out, if it will succeed—this is still a question, but I will not let the play be performed if you refuse to play in it. I have almost no money now and if you refuse to perform I will be, as they say, entirely lost.

February 17, 1903

TO OLGA KNIPPER:

Why are you so happy to play a virtuous part? Virtuous parts are played only by untalented and malicious actresses. Here it is: eat the compliment.

March 1, 1903

TO OLGA KNIPPER:

The paper for the play is laid out on my desk. I have written the title already.

March 5 and 6, 1903

TO OLGA KNIPPER:

In "Cherry Orchard" you will be Varvara Egorovna—Varya, an adopted daughter, twenty-two years old. The part of Varya is very comical. And Stanislavsky's part will also be very comical.† If the play does not come out as I envisage

* Lilina, wife of Konstantin Stanislavsky, played Anya in *The Cherry Orchard.*

† Chekhov hoped that Stanislavsky would play Lopahin.

it, you can slap my forehead with your fist. Stanislavsky's part is comical, so is yours.

March 18, 1903

TO OLGA KNIPPER:

The play, coming to the point, doesn't seem to succeed. One main character is not yet thought through and disturbs—but I think by Easter this person will be clear and I will be freed from all difficulties.

March 21, 1903

TO OLGA KNIPPER:

"Cherry Orchard" will have—I have tried to give it—as few as possible characters; so it will be more intimate.

April 11, 1903

TO OLGA KNIPPER:

Will you have an actress for the part of an elderly lady in "Cherry Orchard"? If not, there will not be a play; I will not write it.

July 28, 1903

TO KONSTANTIN STANISLAVSKY:

My play is not ready; it progresses with difficulty, which I explain by laziness and wonderful weather and the difficulty of the subject. When it is ready, or even before, I will write to you or, better, send you a wire. Your part [Lopahin] it seems came out not bad at all, although I don't want to judge, because generally in reading plays I understand very little.

August 22, 1903

TO VLADIMIR NEMIROVICH-DANCHENKO:

As to my play, "The Cherry Orchard," as of now everything is in good shape. I work on and off. If I am late it will not be too bad; scenically I brought the play down to a minimum; special decor will not be necessary. . . . In the second act I substituted the river with an old chapel and a well. It is quieter so. But in the second act you will give me a real green field, and a road, and an extraordinary distance.

September 2, 1903

TO VLADIMIR NEMIROVICH-DANCHENKO:

My play (if I continue to work as I worked today) will be finished soon, rest assured. Difficult, very difficult it was to write the second act, but apparently it went well. I will call the play a comedy. . . . In my play the part of the mother will be Olga's [Knipper], but who will play the daughter, a girl of seventeen to eighteen, young and delicate, I don't even want to decide. We'll see.

September 15, 1903

TO LILINA:

My dear Maria Petrovna, don't believe anybody; not a living soul has yet read my play. For you I wrote not a "bigot" but a very naive young lady with which, I hope, you will be satisfied. I have almost finished the play but eight or ten days ago I became ill, started to cough, became weak; in one word the same story as last year. It came out not as a drama but as a comedy, and in spots even a farce.

September 20, 1903

TO OLGA KNIPPER:

I am so far away from everything that I begin to lose my spirit. It seems to me that as a writer I have outlived my time and each sentence I write is not good at all and unnecessary.

EXCERPTS FROM CHEKHOV'S LETTERS

September 21, 1903

TO OLGA KNIPPER:

The last act will be gay, but then the whole play is gay and frivolous.

September 23, 1903

TO OLGA KNIPPER:

In comparison with the others the fourth act will be meager in its content, but effective. The end of your part seems to be not bad at all.

September 25, 1903

TO OLGA KNIPPER:

I am writing the fourth act easily and it is apparently well shaped. And if I haven't finished it speedily, it is because I am ailing. It seems to me that in my play—however dull it may be—there is something new. By the way, there is not a single shot in the whole play.

September 27, 1903

TO OLGA KNIPPER:

I have already wired you that the play is finished, that all four acts are written. I am already copying it. The people come out alive, this is true, but how the play goes I don't know. I will send it to you; you'll read it and know for yourself.

September 29, 1903

TO OLGA KNIPPER:

The play is ready but I copy it slowly since I must make changes, think it over, and a couple of spots will be sent unfinished; I put it over for later. You must excuse me. . . . If only you would play the governess in my play! This is the best part; the others I don't like.

EXCERPTS FROM CHEKHOV'S LETTERS

October 2, 1903

TO OLGA KNIPPER:

I write every day, even if it is just a little, but still—I write. I will send you the play, you will read it, and you will see what could have been done under favorable circumstances, that is, being well. But now it is just a shame, writing two lines a day and becoming accustomed to what you write.

October 8, 1903

TO OLGA KNIPPER:

The play goes ahead; today I'll finish the rewrite of Act III and begin on IV. The third act is the least boring, but the second is all in one piece like a cobweb.

October 9, 1903

TO OLGA KNIPPER:

I rewrite the play and will finish soon, I swear. . . . I assure you that each extra day is useful, since my play becomes better and better and all the characters are already clear. I only fear that there are places which the censorship may strike out, and this will be horrible.

October 12, 1903

TO OLGA KNIPPER:

The play is finished, definitely finished and tomorrow evening or at the latest on the morning of the fourteenth will be sent to Moscow. At the same time I will enclose some remarks for you. If changes are needed it seems to me they will not be big. The very worst about the play is that I did not write it at one time but over a long, long time, and a certain heaviness must therefore be felt. . . . How difficult it was for me to write this play!

EXCERPTS FROM CHEKHOV'S LETTERS

October 14, 1903

TO OLGA KNIPPER:

If the play will be produced, you can say that I will make necessary changes. I have time, but I must confess that I am fed up with the play. The house is old, gentleman-like; at one time people used to live there very sumptuously, and this must be felt in the furniture. Varya is somewhat coarse and a little stupid, but very good-hearted.

October 19, 1903

TO OLGA KNIPPER:

Will my play be produced? And if yes—when? . . . Write me also who will play Charlotta. . . . Is it possible that it will be Rayevskaya*? Then it will not be Charlotta, but a noncomical Russian Evdoksia. I didn't write to you yesterday, awaiting your wire. Yesterday late in the evening I got your wire and one from Nemirovich-Danchenko—180 words. Many thanks. I was so afraid. Mainly on account of the second act. . . . It is slow and the character of Trofimov is not quite finished. Trofimov is on and off in exile, thrown out of the university, and how can you show such things.

October 23, 1903

TO OLGA KNIPPER:

You write that Vishnevsky cannot play Gaev. Then who? Stanislavsky? But then who will be Lopahin? . . . Nemirovich writes that there are tears in my play and coarseness. . . . So the actors like Pishchik? I am very glad.

* M. P. Rayevskaya had played Polina in the Moscow Art Theatre's production of *The Sea Gull.*

EXCERPTS FROM CHEKHOV'S LETTERS

October 23, 1903

TO VLADIMIR NEMIROVICH-DANCHENKO:

I would very much like to be in on some rehearsals, just to look. I am afraid that Anya will have a crying tone (somehow you find her similar to Irina). I am afraid that she will be played by a not-young actress. Anya doesn't once cry, never speaks in a crying voice. In the second act she has tears in her eyes, but her tone is gay and lively. Why do you speak in your wire about many crying people in the play? Where are they? Only Varya, but this is only because Varya is a cry-baby in her nature and her tears must not evoke a cheerlessness in the spectator. Often you will find "through tears," but it shows only the expression of the face, not tears. There is not a cemetery in the second act.

October 28, 1903

TO OLGA KNIPPER:

No, I never wanted Ranevskaya to slow down. Only death can slow down such a woman. It may well be that I don't understand what you want to say. It is not difficult to play Ranevskaya; only one must from the very beginning take a right tone, one must find a smile and a manner of laughing, one must know how to dress.

February 27, 1904

TO OLGA KNIPPER:

"Cherry Orchard" is now performed in all the cities; three and four times, and has success; imagine it!

March 24, 1904

TO OLGA KNIPPER:

Tell the actress who plays the maid [Dunyasha] to read the

play in the "Znanie" publication or in the corrected manuscript; then she will know where she has to use powder for her nose, etc. In your copy books everything is in disorder and smeared.

April 10, 1904

TO OLGA KNIPPER:

Why is it that in the playbills and advertisements my play is so tenaciously called drama? Nemirovich and Alekseev [Stanislavsky] see in my play positively not what I wrote; and I am prepared to pledge my word that they both haven't read my play attentively even once.